The Tug: Findu̱ɡ   *̱hip*

As an entrepreneur who helps develop budding entrepreneurs, Barbara Zabawa addresses the initial steps to bringing an idea to life in a practical, easy-to-read format. I recommend this book to all those who are considering starting their own venture. I know Barbara and how creative, smart, and resourceful she is. Truly resilient—as is required of successful entrepreneurs.
—Robert J. Devita, Founder of Common Ground Health Care
and Adjunct Professor at UW—Milwaukee

"The Tug" offers solid, detailed insights into the earliest stages of the entrepreneurship process. Whether you are looking to start a business that sells products or services, or even a podcast, this book will help you get started and feel more confident along the way.
—Michael Barbouche, Founder and CEO of Forward Health Group

So many in our society are searching for meaning in their life. This book serves as an essential guide to find that meaning through entrepreneurship and giving the reader a sense of community as they take their first steps on their entrepreneurial journey so they don't do it alone.
—Angus Nelson, Speaker, Consultant, Coach & host of the Up in Your Business Podcast.

In "The Tug: How to Find Purpose and Joy through Entrepreneurship," Barbara Zabawa offers answers to questions most entrepreneurs will likely have—more importantly, she provides practical how-to advice, heartfelt encouragement, inspiration, and priceless insights from her experience with her own start-ups to address "you don't know what you don't know" topics.
—Michelle Spehr, MA, M.Ed., MCHES ®, CWWPC, CWF

Got an entrepreneurial idea that "tugs" at you but you're not sure where to begin? ... A much-needed book in the self-help genre that gives budding entrepreneurs a practical roadmap to bring their idea to life.
—Laura Putnum, CEO of Motion Infusion and author of *Workplace Wellness that Works*

So many of us are searching for meaning and fulfillment in our lives. This book serves as an essential guide to find that meaning through entrepreneurship. I particularly loved the Valuable First Steps, 2021 Checklists, and Bountiful Resources. I wish I had "The Tug" in my hands when I started my business. I will have it on hand now as a valuable modern resource.
—Jennifer Abernethy, 2x National Author and Entrepreneur,
Founder of SociallyDelivered.com and Mod.Life

"The Tug" is a great one-stop manual for people considering any level of entrepreneurial venture. Barbara generously and authentically shares detailed insights from her own journey and considerations that are critical to the entrepreneurial process. Whether you're pursuing a full-time opportunity or side-gig, these principles apply and will help you every step of the way.
—Rosie Ward, Ph.D., CEO/Co-Founder of Salveo Partners and co-author of
Rehumanizing the Workplace and *How to Build a Thriving Culture at Work*

Barbara Zabawa's important book helps address the "Tug" so many of us feel the call to do something differ-ent from what we have done—to innovate, disrupt, and fix something we see as broken. For some, this "Tug" will lead them to create new products or services; for others, it will lead them to create change in the social sector and for some perhaps do what they have always done in a different way. Using her own personal stories and experiences, Zabawa leads on a journey to embrace and not be afraid of that small voice that we hear yearning to do something new, scary, and powerful.
—Suzanne McKechnie Klahr, Esq., CEO, Mayacamas Partners LLC

THE TUG

FINDING PURPOSE AND JOY
THROUGH ENTREPRENEURSHIP

Other books by Barbara Zabawa

Rule the Rules of Workplace Wellness Programs

Law for Fitness Managers and Exercise Professionals

THE TUG

FINDING PURPOSE AND JOY
THROUGH ENTREPRENEURSHIP

BARBARA J. ZABAWA, JD, MPH

Henschel
HAUS
publishing, inc.
Milwaukee, Wisconsin

The information in this book is for educational purposes only and does not constitute legal advice or guarantee any results.

Published by
HenschelHAUS Publishing, Inc.
www.HenschelHAUSbooks.com
Milwaukee, Wisconsin
Please contact the publisher for quantity discounts.

ISBN: 978159598-821-8
E-ISBN: 978159598-822-5
LCCN: 2021931182

Cover art by Vivian Zabawa-Lodholz

Printed in the United States of America

To my husband Branden, my Champion
and
to my kids Patrick and Vivian, my "Why."

TABLE OF CONTENTS

INTRODUCTION

LET ME SHARE A SECRET: YOU KNOW that feeling you have, or maybe it's an inner voice, telling you to do something different with your life? The one that creeps into your conscience day and night? I call it the "tug." Well, the tug is real. I have felt it, and much to the protests and objections from others, I followed it. And I couldn't feel more fulfilled.

I first felt the tug during my final years working as a lawyer for a big law firm. I didn't know exactly why, but a nagging little voice kept telling me I was meant for something different. It was frustrating to sense this "tug" away from a secure job where I had just succeeded in making partner. For many lawyers, I had just achieved the ultimate milestone and should celebrate. But the tug was still there, so I was unhappy and restless. I didn't know what to do about it, or why the tug was even bothering me in the first place.

Pay attention to that tug. Even though it may not seem like it, it is leading you somewhere that is full of excitement and fulfillment.

This book is for individuals who yearn for something more. Who have ideas but don't know what to do with them, or if it's even worth pursuing them. I am one of those "serial entrepreneurs" who is full of ideas. I struggle with finding time to implement them all, and must prioritize them so I can be as effective and fulfilled as possible. But therein lies the difference between me at the big law firm, and me now.

When I finally took the leap to entrepreneurship, that "tug" I felt for so many years disappeared. I still feel frustration and disappointment in my ideas, but the overarching purpose of my life has become more clear and my internal compass is steady. And though I have not yet achieved the same level of financial success as many start-ups you read about in the news, I am able to pay my bills, be in control of my destiny and feel joy in what I do, which is priceless.

1

Why did I write this book?

I wrote this book to help people who, like me, feel a "tug" to take their life in a new, exciting direction but haven't the faintest clue about entrepreneurship. I want to show you how to do what you love. You see, I think often times the tug is leading you toward entrepreneurship. Entrepreneurship is scary, especially for people like me who have held secure jobs all their life. Well, let me tell you another little secret, those jobs are not always secure. In fact, in my experience, jobs are volatile and can be gone in an instant without much notice. I have seen so many friends fall victim to corporate restructuring, company closures, or just unbearable conditions where the choice between sticking it out or keeping your sanity, sanity must win.

One of my favorite comedians, Jim Carrey, gave a commencement speech and referenced his father, who could have been a great comedian, but believed such a dream was impossible. Instead he made a conservative choice and took a "safe" job as an accountant only to lose that job. In his inspiring speech, Jim Carrey said: "I learned many great lessons from my father, not the least of which is that you can fail at what you don't want, so you might as well take a chance on doing what you love."[1]

That speech was all over the Internet the year I started my law firm. It inspired me to take the leap. Perhaps it will inspire you.

Using my own three entrepreneurial ventures as examples when most appropriate, I walk you through the steps of becoming an entrepreneur. As a budding entrepreneur myself, I've read my share of career development and business success books. I've also watched videos by successful entrepreneurs to gain nuggets of wisdom. I love hearing about other people's success stories, particularly when I am starting my own new venture. When your life is thrown into chaos because of something new, whether done purposefully or involuntarily, you feel vulnerable,

---

[1] Jim Carrey, Commencement Speech to Maharishi University, June 13, 2014, available at https://www.youtube.com/watch?v=q2rVDCrt6QY&ab_channel=WonderJam (last visited October 6, 2020).

alone, and often have many questions. That's when self-help books and videos are all the more coveted.

Often those books and videos are authored by individuals who are years into the future from when they first set out to achieve their ambitions. They have found success, and now they are sharing their wisdom with you. There is certainly value in that. Or, the books or blog posts try to address early stage entrepreneurship, but they consider early stage the first few years of a venture. There is also value in that. Or they assume you work in Silicon Valley and want to become the next Steve Jobs. There is a lot to admire and learn from that as well.

I believe, however, that there is a group of people out there who like me, just want to quiet the inner voice that keeps them up at night. They are in search of their true purpose at this phase in their life and just want to hear that quieting that voice is indeed possible through entrepreneurship and they would like a roadmap on how to do it. So, this book is about learning from your peer, me, who is going through the very beginnings of a new venture and has had some success with two others previously. When I say I'm beginning a new venture, I mean the first few weeks or months of implementing an idea. Hearing from a peer who is at this stage as their venture unfolds can offer important lessons and create a sense of camaraderie, like a support group.

Indeed, learning from your peers offers details about the experience, as it happens, that are often lost in the retrospective wisdom often found in the self-help books and videos I mention above. For those of us who are taking their first entrepreneurial steps, hearing the details can be very helpful. Experiencing the highs and lows during the first year of a new venture is more tolerable if you experience it with a comrade.

As Duke University researchers Victor Bennett and Aaron Chatterji point out, entrepreneurial research offers very little insight into the early stages of entrepreneurship. But it is in these early stages where crucial decisions are made as to whether to continue pursuing your idea. Many self-help books aim to provide you inspirational courage, but lack in practical know-how. Sometimes those self-help books offer advice concerning stages of idea or ambition implementation that are years away, such as scaling your venture, or building a strong company culture. Information like that, although valuable, is not very helpful in the very beginning stages of a new venture. Especially for individuals new to entrepreneurship. And especially for those of us without high-powered funding or connections. This book tries to change that.

When I started writing this book, I read an article about the founder of the information technology news publication *The Information*, Jessica Lessin. She is doing important work by exposing how information technology is taking over everything, and not always in a good way. But she was able to start her successful publication with her own money; her family, as well as her husband's family have financial resources of which most of us only dream. I'm here to tell you I am not from a family with financial resources. I am the first in my family to attend college. And, I provide financial support to my parents, not the other way around.

Despite the lack of family financial backing, like many of the readers of this book, I am starting my latest venture called Pursesuitz without any financial inheritance or investor backing. It is not my first venture. About six years earlier I started my own law firm, the Center for Health and Wellness Law, LLC, something that was never on my career bucket list. Yet, I felt compelled to try. I attribute the move to the tug, nudging me to do something else, something brave. I had been working as in-house counsel at the time, after having just made partner in a large law firm. When one of my former clients begged me to come back to private practice, the thought of opening my own law firm jumped into my mind. Once I thought of starting my own law firm, the thought refused to escape my mind. I knew that if I didn't at least try, I would regret it later in life.

Before my law firm, I had also started a venture called Lemonspark. Lemonspark grew out of an unexpected loss almost ten years before I started my law firm. It was my first real "lemon" in life, and I felt alone, afraid, and without hope. I longed for a community of people who could understand the deep sadness, anger and fear I felt, but could also help me feel hopeful and inspired. In terms of my life's purpose, I needed to know "why" this lemon happened to me. None of the support groups I found could help me answer that question, so I started Lemonspark to seek out stories from people who had overcome life's lemons through starting a venture that wouldn't have existed but for that lemon.

My latest venture, Pursesuitz, definitely feels like another idea I must try or face regret later in life. The inspiration for creating clothes with functional pockets grew out of personal frustration with lugging around a purse most of my life. As I discuss in this book, the idea of a blouse with pockets appeared, I took some action initially, and then sat on it for a while until I felt compelled to move forward, which at the time of writing this book was only a few months ago. The idea of writing a book about my entrepreneurial experience arose as I thought about how useful it would be to memorialize my entrepreneurial journey for the benefit of future entrepreneurs. I have started enough ventures, both service-related and now a product-based venture, that the details of my experience might inspire someone to heed the call of their own "tug" and help guide them through the process. Indeed, this book represents what Pursesuitz is about: *to give people tools to pursue their dreams with more freedom and ease.*

As you take steps toward finding your purpose, doors will open. Those doors may have been open to you the whole time, but until you start paying attention to that tug, you won't notice them or seek them out.

CHAPTER ONE
LISTEN TO YOUR "TUG"

IF YOU ARE WILLING TO TAKE A RISK in response to a "tug," you are on your way to entrepreneurship. According to Dictionary.com, an "entrepreneur" is *"a person who organizes and manages any enterprise, especially a business, usually with considerable initiative and risk."*

I believe entrepreneurship encompasses more than just starting a business. I believe it is about putting yourself out there with no real safety net. It's about taking a leap of faith and pouring yourself into a venture because you believe in it, even when others sit back and wonder if you really have the guts and drive to follow through.

Why are you feeling your tug? Your tug might stem from an idea to solve a problem, or just a feeling that you were meant for something different and you aren't living out your true destiny. Perhaps you are feeling frustrated or anxious, or life handed you a lemon and you are trying to make lemonade from it. Whatever your reason, I strongly believe that the tug is life's magnetic pull toward your true purpose. Your ambition—your initiative—is what causes you to take risks in exchange for finding that purpose. That purpose may translate into more knowledge, more impact, more fulfillment, more meaning, more authority or power, or a combination of these. But even more important than any of those things, finding your purpose gives you joy. Feeling joy in what you do can propel you down unimaginable paths and make life more exciting and fulfilling.

All entrepreneurs start with an idea. Often, that idea aims to solve a problem or fill a gap that no one else is stepping up to solve or fill. In my case, or at least my most recent case, that problem is the lack of functional, secure pockets in women's clothing, eliminating the need for women to carry a purse or handbag. For me, carrying a purse has become an intolerable burden. It seems to always get in the way, like at the grocery store, a sporting event, concert, movie theater, or in my car, to name a few examples. If it's not getting in the way, then it has been contributing to me missing phone calls on my smart phone. Because my clothes have no functional pockets, I put my phone in my purse. But, especially at home or when I worked in an office, my purse wasn't always with me. If my phone rings and I am nowhere near my purse, I miss the phone call. For someone who uses her cell phone for business, missing phone calls is perilous.

My personal frustration with this problem compelled me to find a solution, which is how Pursesuitz was born. The concept of Pursesuitz is to make women's clothing or "suits" serve as a purse so that women can free themselves from the burden of carrying a purse. I am designing that solution as I write this book, which you will hear more about.

Before Pursuitz, my entrepreneurial ventures included starting a law firm, the Center for Health and Wellness Law, LLC, as well as Lemonspark, which started out as a nonprofit but is now a podcast. The reason why I started each of those ventures was to fill a gap in the marketplace. However, the spark that motivated me to start those ventures was very different from Pursesuitz. With Pursesuitz, I just felt exhausted from not having a satisfying option to carrying a purse. I started the Center for Health and Wellness Law, however, because I was unsatisfied with my career and needed something different. The tug was much stronger than with Pursesuitz.

Lemonspark came into existence because I needed a community of individuals who were not only handed lemons in life, such as divorce, illness, or tragic loss, but found meaning in those lemons through entrepreneurship. Hearing those stories at a time when I felt incredible sadness was very therapeutic. But enough about my ventures. Let's turn to yours.

What is Your Idea?

Your idea can take the form of a product, like Pursesuitz, or it can take the form of providing a unique service, or a service to a group of individuals with unmet needs, or a service in a unique way or from a unique perspective. Your idea can be an ambition to do business in a different way, to expand your client base, or create something spectacularly new. Whatever your idea is, in order to get "noticed" by those you are trying to attract, you and your product or service must stand out. It must be unique in some aspect.

So how can you stand out? It starts with wanting to solve a problem or fill a gap. Many of you may have already identified your idea, but others may still be searching. If you are in the latter group, start searching for it. What is your angle that will set you apart from the rest of the pack? There is always "the rest of the pack" from which you must differentiate yourself. There are other professionals in your workplace, other start-ups, other creative geniuses. Ideally, your idea or ambition should sprout from your authentic self, but, it doesn't necessarily have to achieve a goal. For example, your ambition may be to work harder than everyone else. If you work longer and harder than everyone else who is aiming for the same goal as you, that work ethic will set you apart and get you noticed. Your tenacious work ethic may fill the need faced by your firm or company of having dedicated, capable employees. That is terrific, as long as you continue to find your life fulfilling and don't burn out.

For those of you looking to start a business or build a customer base for a business, your idea should aim to solve a problem. If your idea is to start a business, ask yourself what problems do you face in your daily life that you wish would be solved? If you reflect long enough, I bet you'll discover something that annoys you and that you can come up with a solution to that annoying problem. Chances are, if something annoys you, it probably annoys others as well. Those others are your "tribe," a concept I discuss further in Chapter Nine.

If your idea is to build a customer base, a must for any professional career advancement, you must consider what is unique about your service offering compared to your competition. Are your services more client-friendly? More up to date? More technically savvy? More niche? Think about what special angle you can provide within your service expertise, which might be legal, accounting, engineering, financial, advertising, marketing, social media, or some other important service.

When I started my law firm, I decided to specialize in a very narrow practice area with which no other lawyers identified: wellness law. In fact, I invented the practice area and secured the domain name: wellnesslaw.com. To this day, when you Google "wellness law," the most common results concern wellness programs that are offered to lawyers inside law firms. The legal industry, as well as Google, have yet to recognize wellness law as a legal practice area, like employment law or criminal law. But that is ok. Because I created this niche practice area, whenever I attend industry conferences, I am the only lawyer in the room. Previously, when I had identified as a "health lawyer," I would attend conferences and have to compete with many other lawyers chasing the same potential clients. Inventing a new practice area or way of delivering services gives you market advantage. Go find it, if you haven't already. To give you some inspiration, here is how the idea of Pursesuitz came to be.

Your Idea and the Superconscious Mind

Ultimately, your idea is likely to be something that is already stored in your superconscious mind. The concept of a "superconscious mind" derives from the timeless book by Florence Scovel Shinn called *The Game of Life and How to Play It*. It was written in 1925, so some of the language is dated, but the concepts are still relevant. According to Ms. Scovel Shinn, the superconscious mind is the "God Mind" and is the realm of perfect ideas. It is where your Divine Design, or true purpose, resides. Ms. Scovel Shinn states: "There is a place that you are to fill and no one else can fill, something you are to do, which no one else can do."

Your superconscious mind holds the perfect picture of your idea, or your true purpose. Ms. Scovel Shinn explains that this perfect picture usually flashes across your conscious mind as an unattainable ideal or "something too good to be true." But what appears to be an unattainable ideal is in fact your true destiny.

I saw such flashes of success for Lemonspark, the Center for Health and Wellness Law, and Pursesuitz. For Lemonspark, I see a "go-to" show for people who are hurting and who want to find inspiration, hope and a sense of belonging. The show is so popular that people start using the word "Lemonspark" to describe a situation where someone takes a tragic event and turns it into something meaningful.

I see the Center for Health and Wellness Law as a law firm that employs a dozen attorneys who specialized not only in health and wellness law, but also policy and consulting. The firm serves as an indispensable resource to health and wellness providers, who feel more empowered to help others achieve their best self. I also see the health law community acknowledging "wellness law" as a new, interesting legal practice area.

Finally, my vision for Pursesuitz is that my "hero" product, the Pocketwear Tank Top, will be an essential item for many women, particularly those who do not like to carry purses everywhere. I have dreams of my product appearing on TV and promoted by celebrities because it is so useful and comfortable. Most importantly, I see Pursesuitz giving me an opportunity to branch outside of legal work and exercise my creative side.

An Example of How Ideas are Born: Pursesuitz

I formulated the idea of Pursesuitz because I was, and continue to be, annoyed with purses. I envisioned a world in which I was free from carrying a purse. Purses are heavy and they hurt my shoulder. They get in my way in my car, at restaurants, at the grocery store or when I am at an event like a concert, theater or sporting event or dance party. Purses are something that I can forget, or lose at the hands of a thief. They are something I need others to watch if I want to be "hands free" (like on the dance floor). They are something that if dropped can reveal intimate secrets all over the floor. Most annoyingly, purses are something that distinguishes me as a woman, which is particularly problematic as a professional woman trying to advance her career.

When I worked for a large law firm, I observed my male counterparts breeze into the office, hands in their pockets, sometimes carrying a briefcase, sometimes not, but always seeming to be unburdened by a heavy bag. They would stop by my office to say "hello" and chat for a bit until they made their way to their own space. My female counterparts, if they stopped at all, would inevitably have to find a place to rest their bags, usually a purse and a work bag, as those bags get heavy after being held for a while. If they didn't stop to say hello, I might not see them for the rest of the day, as once they got to their offices to drop off their stuff, they inevitably got sucked into checking voicemail or email and starting their workday. I enjoyed the brief chitchats with my male counterparts because I usually learned something and it made the workday more pleasant. I began to wonder, *Are handbags holding us women back?*

Then, in a rare opportunity to see one of my cases being argued before the United States Supreme Court, I realized how unfortunate women were for relying on purses in professional situations. Before leaving for the courthouse, my male colleagues and I were instructed to leave our bags at the office as they were not allowed inside the courtroom. What they forgot to mention is that we also needed our identification cards in order to be admitted inside the courtroom. I didn't learn that until we drove the several miles to the courthouse and walked up to security.

Because I carried a purse, all my essential items, like my wallet and driver's license, were in my purse, which I had dutifully left behind at the office. Panicked, I had to catch a taxi back to the office, dig through my purse for my identification, and take a taxi back to the courthouse. Fortunately, I arrived in time for the oral argument, but I felt embarrassed and frustrated at my dependency on my purse. My male colleagues, of course, did not have that issue, because their essentials like identification cards are always on their person, in their pockets. The idea of Pursesuitz began to percolate through my head.

It would be several years, and many more frustrating moments of lugging around a purse, before I took any action in making Pursesuitz come to life, which I will discuss shortly.

Can You Have Multiple Ideas or Purposes in Life, or is there only One True Purpose?

I believe wholeheartedly you can have multiple purposes in life, just as you play multiple roles. For example, as a woman, you may play wife, mother, employee, daughter, sister, volunteer, supervisor, and so on. Each role is important and a chance to play out one of your purposes in life. I believe the same can be said for your vocation. You don't have to settle for only one vocational role in your life.

Now, before I go any further, I will say that trying to fit multiple purposes in your life is a challenge. You can feel very overwhelmed much of the time, and yearn for a more simple, singular-purpose life. I know I have felt that way too many times to count. I have wrestled with trying to figure out which one of my ideas (my law firm, Lemonspark, and Pursesuitz) is really my one and only "true" purpose. I thought that I needed to choose one if I was ever going to get to the pinnacle of that vocation.

Over time, however, as I struggled to pick the right path for me, I found I didn't need to choose. Ben Franklin did not settle for just one vocation. He was a printer, postmaster, statesman, inventor, author, and philanthropist, just to name a few of his professional accomplishments. When he saw a problem, he set out to fix it, even if he had no formal education in the subject.[2] He was self-taught, and his integrity, hard work and perseverance propelled him to success. So next time you feel like you must choose, think twice if that is really necessary. Perhaps you are

---

[2] Blaine McCormick, *Ben Franklin: America's Original Entrepreneur, 1788* (Kindle edition).

like Ben Franklin, who contributed to the greater good in many different professional areas.

The truth is, I love all my ideas, and I will pursue them all until they naturally evolve the way they are meant to evolve. As long as I gave into enjoying the journey of nurturing each idea, at my own pace, then what was the harm in moving forward with them all? As soon as it no longer brings me joy, however, it will be time to pack up and be done.

Naming Your Idea or Business

It is not necessary to put a name to your business idea immediately. For many of us, a creative name can just pop into your head at any moment, so don't feel rushed to find a name. But you should write down your idea and create a folder or file, whether on paper or electronically, to keep thoughts related to your idea in one place. For Pursesuitz, I created a separate folder on my MacBook. When I come across articles or photos related to my idea, I store them in this folder.

The name for "Pursesuitz" came to me after playing with some words. Because I initially wanted to focus on professional women (or "ambitious" women) who wanted to pursue their goals with more freedom, I thought of the word "pursuit," which contains the word "suit," a typical fashion item worn by professional women. Also because I was frustrated with purses and want to replace them with functional pockets, I used the word "purse," also phonetically part of the word "pursue." By researching online both on Google and my state's business website to see if the name idea was available, I saw that the word "pursuits" was taken. But, if I used the actual word "purse" and added a "z" instead of an "s" at the end of suit, the combination was available both as a business name and as a domain name with a ".com" ending. So, I secured the domain name and sat on it for a couple of years more.

> As a tip, changing up a common word with a different spelling can help with trademarking that name as well.

14

Should You Name Your Business After You?

It depends. Many people name their business after themselves because it's tradition (e.g., most law firms are named after their founding partners), or because it's easy. If you have a unique name, it's easy to lay claim to the name for your business. You might have an easier time securing the domain name and trademark. But, if you name your business after you, your name will be forever associated with your business. That might be fun if your business takes off and people marvel at meeting the person behind the brand, but what if you want to switch gears someday? Or what if you value anonymity? Then, it might be better to name your business after something that is not associated with you or your family tree. According to some sources, it is easier to sell a business that is not named after the founder. So, if you dream of one day cashing in from your business, building a brand around a name that is not associated with you personally may make your business more attractive to future buyers.

It's About Fulfillment, Not Financial Windfalls

Sometimes our ideas start out grand, which is wonderful for a long-term view. But a monumental idea can be overwhelming. Nothing can stop an idea in its tracks faster than feeling overwhelmed. I attribute a lot of this overwhelm to pressure to succeed financially. You might think that if your idea is not the next "pet rock" or Facebook, then it is not worth pursuing. That couldn't be farther from the truth. Your "tug" is not necessarily leading you to riches and fame. It's leading you to your life's purpose. If you follow it and feel fulfilled, is that not enough? So, if you start to feel overwhelmed, don't despair. Remember the journey itself can be fulfilling, and you control the timeline.

So, once you have your idea, to keep it manageable, it's best to scale it back into smaller milestones. It's ok if you don't have all the milestones mapped out to the end goal. I believe those will be filled in as you move forward. In fact, I think it's impossible to have every step in clear focus when you first decide to bring your idea into reality. Life is full of surprises, so it's important to stay nimble. But to have a few milestones as part of your vision at the outset can keep you moving toward your goal.

I would like Pursesuitz to someday have an entire collection of clothing: pants, skirts, blouses, and jackets. But, we'll see how my first product performs in the marketplace. I would also like Lemonspark to offer online classes and retreats to help those trying to find meaning from their traumatic experience. But, I'll start with my podcast and see how much interest that generates. As Sarah Blakely, founder of Spanx, recommends, start with a "hero" product or service and work on achieving success for that before expanding to other products or services.

Once you identify your hero product or service, start writing down your plans and putting them into action.

Taking the First Step

Once you settle on your idea, the most courageous thing you will do next is actually start putting it into action. I believe this is where most people with great ideas fall short. They don't make their idea a reality. I understand why: it can be time-consuming and very expensive. But I also believe that you can find ways to make it work, because as I mention throughout this book, *you control the timeline*. That is such an obvious, but overlooked fact about entrepreneurship. You don't have to give up everything else to pursue your idea. You can work at a pace that fits within your life's schedule. The fact that you chip away at it is more than most people will do. So don't criticize yourself if you can't or don't want to go "all in" from the get-go. And be prepared to pivot as you go, because each step you take toward achieving your goal will teach you something that you did not know or expect. This is what happened with Pursesuitz.

My hero product for Pursesuitz started as a two-layer blouse with functional pockets. Once I had my vision for the hero product, I purchased a few clothing items to get a "feel" for the fabric and shape of the inner layer that I would like to use. My husband Branden, who sews (I do not), made a prototype using the fabric I found. Based on this very

16

preliminary research, my idea seemed like it would work. But I needed to test it further.

Because I do not work in the fashion industry, I had no idea what to do next. So, I started to enlist the help of others. I quickly learned that because of my lack of experience, I would need to find a partner or mentor who had the experience I lacked to help me move forward. So, I researched fashion resources for start-ups and found a few places that specialize in helping newbies like me get from a fashion idea to a prototype to manufacturing multiple items.

I didn't settle on the first few places I found. Instead, I continued to research options. When I contacted some of these individuals, they pointed me to additional options, which I kept calling until I found the one that seemed like the right fit. As frequently happens when faced with a lot of options, you instinctively know "the one" when you encounter it.

Lauren, my fashion designer consultant, has been terrific. She has led me through the process of designing a clothing product to production and every stage in between. I also found a market consultant by talking with my neighbor, who happened to know this consultant used to own a clothing store in town. I reached out, and Deneen instantly became an incredible resource for me. She helped me conduct several focus groups of my target audience: professional women. I was not prepared for what I learned from those focus groups, as I explain in Chapter Eight. But the information proved invaluable, and made me rethink my hero product.

The point I want to make here is that there are a lot of people out there with the expertise you may not have to help make your idea a reality, and maybe even better than you may have envisioned it. I cover more about finding your team in Chapter Ten. Regardless, you don't need to be the expert. As an entrepreneur, your role is to be captain of the ship and assemble the right team to make the ship go. You set the course, and everyone else takes their cues from you. Granted, if the waters you are charting (to keep with the high-seas analogy) are unfamiliar, you may not be sure which way to go. Lean on your experienced team members for their thoughts until you get comfortable in your shoes, which you will. At that point, you will be ready to take over many of the decisions that you previously delegated to your teammates.

So here's another secret: as an entrepreneur, you are in as much control as you want to be. You control the timeline and the funds you want to spend. If you feel the urge to slow down or stop along the way, you can! It's perfectly fine to do so. Life happens. Entrepreneurship is about taking control of your life and destiny. You get to say when, where, how, and most importantly, *why* you are living the life you lead. You don't need to measure up to or please anyone but yourself.

This is my hope for you as you develop and implement your idea. Keep pressing on, despite the inevitable bumps in the road, including self-doubt, which I cover in the next chapter.

CHECKLIST FOR FORMULATING AND SOLIDIFYING YOUR AMBITION OR IDEA:

❏ Take your time on finding a name for your idea; let the creative process flow naturally.

❏ When you land on a name, research its availability on Google, website hosting sites like hostmonster.com, and your state's department of financial institutions to see if the domain name and name are available.

❏ If your preferred name is not available, see if you can change up the spelling to make it available.

❏ Consider trademarking your name if you plan to go into business using that name.

❏ Think big, but act in baby steps; break up your monumental idea into manageable steps.

❏ Make your first step your "hero" step.

❏ Write down your plan to achieve the hero.

❏ Enlist the help of others when necessary.

❏ Start implementing your "hero" plan.

❏ Remember, you are in control of your timeline and resources.

CHAPTER TWO

OVERCOME SELF-DOUBT

A father said to his daughter: You graduated with honors, here is a car that I acquired many years ago. But before I give it to you, take it to the used car lot downtown and tell them I want to sell it and see how much they offer you.

The daughter went to the used car lot, returned to her father and said "They offered me $1,000 because it looks very worn out."

The father said, "Take it to the pawn shop."

The daughter went to the pawn shop, returned to her father and said "The pawn shop offered $100 because it is a very old car."

The father asked his daughter to go to a car club and show them the car. The daughter took the car to the club, returned and told her father, "Some people in the club offered $100,000 for it since it is a Nissan Skyline R32, an iconic car and sought after by many."

The father said to his daughter, "I wanted you to know that the right place values you the right way."

If you are not valued, do not be angry, it means you are in the wrong place. Those who know your value are those who appreciate you.

Never stay in a place where no one sees your value.

—Author unknown

THIS MEME CIRCULATED THROUGH SOCIAL media in 2020. Regardless of its veracity, it adeptly makes a point: find your tribe and they will see your idea's true worth. Finding your tribe is key to overcoming self-doubt. Self-doubt creeps in when you hear criticism or maybe unenthusiastic responses. It's ok. As one of my bosses used to say, "Work with the willing." Many people will not be worth your effort to convince your idea has value. But I'd bet there is a tribe of people out there who will need very little convincing. Once you find them, focus on them. It will renew and sustain your belief in your idea.

I believe in my ideas wholeheartedly. Yet, I still face moments of self-doubt. In fact, my Pursesuitz idea has made it really easy to doubt myself. My formal training and education have been in public health and law, not fashion design, much less the business of fashion. Sure, as a lawyer I may be able to navigate some of the legal and business aspects of operating this new enterprise, but the vast majority of the fashion world is absolutely foreign to me. Other than working in a women's retail shop while in college, I have no experience with clothing design or manufacture. So, there have been moments when I have questioned whether this venture is a good idea. This was especially true after conducting my focus groups to get feedback on my first Pursesuitz prototypes. Here are some photos of me modeling the first prototypes:

Can you see the excitement in my face? The first two photos show the two different outer layer styles. They each have slits in the sides that easily access the pockets in the inner layer, shown in the third photo.

You can see that I have all my "essential items" stuffed into the inner layer pockets, like my phone, wallet, keys, and a Chapstick. The outer layer was designed to conceal the inner layer pockets for a clean, professional look.

The focus group attendees were lukewarm about the idea, at best. They didn't like the two layers, didn't like the beige color of the base layer, didn't like the heaviness of the fabric for the outer layers, and probably most disturbingly, didn't like the idea of giving up their purses. What?!?! It was shocking to hear such different attitudes toward my product, my baby, than I had been telling myself all these months leading up to the focus groups. I was not mentally prepared for negative reviews.

After hearing the criticism about my two-layer blouse idea, I felt deflated. It was a classic case of hearing only the bad, and not paying attention to any of the good that came out of the focus groups. My self-doubt overtook me and I began thinking of throwing in the towel.

Then, I spoke to a dear friend, Rhonda Ware, who reached out to me on social media because she was curious about this new activity she had been seeing me post. She coincidentally works as a business/career coach, so she heard the anxiety in my voice when I started explaining my feelings of defeat about Pursesuitz. She offered to coach me through a few sessions, and by the second session, she restored my faith in my idea.

She forced me to remember why I had gone down this entrepreneurial road in the first place: to give women who were frustrated by purses an option. There were women out there who were like me; they just weren't in those focus groups that I conducted. Well, most of the women in the focus groups were not like me, but some were.

Rhonda helped me recognize the good comments that came out of the focus groups. A few women did like the idea and did hate carrying a purse. Most of the focus group attendees also really liked the shapewear layer and would like it more if the pockets were lower and if the color was black instead of beige. They also suggested that they would be more interested in the product for travel or leisure purposes, not work.

Rhonda helped me overcome my self-doubt by reminding me that my idea wasn't about appealing to everyone. That is a failing proposition from the start. Rather, my idea is about finding my tribe, finding the people who see value in my idea, and focusing my efforts on them. Perhaps over time others might join the tribe, but that is not my concern. My concern is to help people in my tribe find a solution to the lack of options for carrying essential items without a purse. As Rhonda noted, even if my solution helps just one person, it's an idea worth pursuing.

My original vision of having a large fashion company wasn't necessary for me to feel fulfilled. All that was necessary was for me to put that solution out into the world so others could benefit, no matter how many or few people that would be.

With that renewed purpose, I re-evaluated my idea and decided to incorporate many of the recommendations and comments made by the focus group attendees into a new, scaled-down hero product. I focused on the inner shapewear layer only. I made it black instead of beige. I gave it a "V" neckline and embroidered a logo on the garment so women had the option of wearing it as a standalone piece or under whatever type of shirt they wanted. I lowered the pockets to make it easy to reach into the pockets when lifting up any outer shirt a woman decides to wear over the inner layer.

The best part of all these changes? I liked the hero product even better than the first version. It was so much more comfortable and versatile. I could wear it underneath a t-shirt, sweatshirt, blouse, or just by itself. I was so relieved that the second iteration was so much better than the first, and for the first time, felt really proud of my accomplishment. And this was before I even sold a single one!

When you have your moments of self-doubt, which you inevitably will, ask yourself these questions about implementing your idea: "If not me, who?" "If not now, when?" And most importantly, "Who will benefit from my idea?"

Overcome Self-Doubt

Here is a photo of me wearing Version Number Two of my hero product. You can order yours at www.pursesuitz.com.

As Sara Blakely, founder of Spanx, states in her Masterclass, "Everyone in his or her lifetime has a million-dollar idea, but are you willing to take the next step? Even if we fail, we will still learn something valuable about ourselves and the environment in which we work. And, we can be satisfied with the experience of giving it a try." (Sara Blakely teaches self-made entrepreneurship, Masterclass.com)

Besides believing in yourself and in your idea, having champions can also help you overcome self-doubt. For me, my husband acts as my champion. Whenever I question my path, he sets me straight. Usually my self-doubt surfaces when I learn something new about the fashion industry; such foreign concepts inevitably make me feel unsure about forging ahead with my idea. When those feelings of self-doubt appear, I turn to my husband, who inevitably reminds me that if anyone can do it, I can. He thinks I'm amazing, and it's usually that little ego boost that helps me swipe away the self-doubt and keep moving forward.

A champion could be anyone who will listen, respond honestly, understands your desire to take risks, but not steal your idea. In essence, your champion must be trustworthy. This could be a family member, friend, co-worker, or even a pet. A mentor can be a terrific champion too, but with older, wiser mentors, I suggest proceeding with caution.

A Word About Mentors

Ever since the breakthrough book *Lean In* by Sheryl Sandberg came out, a lot of attention has been paid to the importance of mentors, especially for professional women. At my previous law firm, the female lawyers read *Lean In* and talked about it as a group. But the book glorifies mentors at the expense of acknowledging potential pitfalls with expecting a mentor to be a champion for ambitious goals. Thus, I argue that what entrepreneurs really need to advance their idea is a champion. A champion may also be a mentor, but a mentor will not necessarily be a champion. A champion understands your desire to take risks and is willing to help you succeed. Mentors may not be the best resource for emotional support or career success.

If your mentor is extremely conservative or risk-averse, he or she will feed your self-doubt. This has happened to me several times in my life with older, wiser mentors. The first was when I thought I wanted to go to dental school. At that time, and probably even still today, most dentists were male. The idea of a female dentist was novel. An aunt of mine, who was also my godmother and who as a child I respected, rejected the idea of a woman dentist when I told her my aspiration. I was a very young adult and unfortunately, too easily swayed by her comment, so I nixed the idea of dental school.

I shake my head that I placed so much value on her opinion back then. I could have used a book like this at that moment; perhaps I would have ignored her comment and pressed forward anyway. If any of you reading this have had a similar dismissal of your idea by someone you thought was your champion, don't heed their advice. Instead, recognize that some individuals are not meant to be entrepreneurs. They are not willing to take risks or view the world in a new way. They may have biases or even feelings of envy that get in the way of their ability to support you. They are not your champions.

The other time I thought my mentor had my back was when I started my law firm in 2014. Before I took the leap, I shared the idea with one of my most trusted mentors. While somewhat supportive of my idea, she was also very rational and much wiser than me in most things. Her rational side cautioned against venturing out on my own as I had just started a new in-house legal position only six months earlier. She thought the better path would be to wait another six months before starting out on my own. That way I could better prepare financially and administratively for my next step. It had been decades since she started her own nonprofit. She was now retired, after working over thirty years at the same University and happily collecting a pension. A secure retirement was her world at the moment.

My mentor's words were wise, but they didn't resonate with my gut instinct. Which is another lesson entrepreneurs should learn: when to trust your gut versus taking sage advice. It's tough, because 20/20 hindsight may prove your gut instinct wrong and the person who gave you the sage advice correct. But then again, that is the risk inherent in all entrepreneurial ventures. Entrepreneurs must have a certain amount of fearlessness to pursue their ideas in the first place.

Let your gut instinct be your compass. Listen to sage advice, maybe use it to pivot if it makes sense, but in the end, if you truly, wholeheartedly believe in your idea, your gut instinct will likely defeat any well-intentioned advice.

This is all to say that if your belief in your idea is strong enough, not much will defeat it, not even self-doubt or doubt imposed by another person.

Not only can mentors fail at nurturing your entrepreneurial spirit, sometimes they can downright sabotage your idea or ambition. Choosing as a mentor another ambitious person, especially one who is inherently a competitor, can jeopardize your goals. When I was aiming to make partner at the last law firm in which I worked before I went in-house, my mentor, a female partner who had been on the firm's board of directors, did nothing to help me achieve my goal. This was because she had her own goals, and my goal of making partner that year stood in the way of her own ambition to work remotely. Working remotely was a big ask for the firm, and because some male partners were opposed to promoting me to partner (for no other reason than gender bias), my mentor failed me as a champion. Achieving her goal outweighed me achieving mine. Without any true champion, my bid for partnership did not occur that year.

Yet, I believed in myself and my worthiness as a future partner of the firm, so I didn't give up. But I no longer relied on my supposed mentor because I no longer trusted her. A year later, I made partner, and a year after that, I started the Center for Health and Wellness Law.

The lesson about good mentors for entrepreneurs is that they may not make the best champions for your idea. Mentors may be great for advice and learning, but they will not be champions unless they truly have faith in you and have your back. To be effective in that way, your mentor must be secure in his or her own position, and not a competitor to your idea. If your mentor feels any vulnerability to her own ambitions, those will take precedence over yours. If your idea is really breaking the mold, your own strength and belief in your idea is what will truly pull you through moments of self-doubt. Thus, an emotional support person or persons may be the best kind of champions—the beings who can remind you of your purpose and calm the waters when they get a bit choppy.

Overcome Self-Doubt

CHECKLIST FOR OVERCOMING SELF-DOUBT:

❑ Belief in your idea is the best antidote to self-doubt.

❑ Continuing to take steps toward implementing your idea, even if very small and even in the face of criticism, keeps opening doors of opportunity that can strengthen your belief in your idea.

❑ Emotional support beings, whether family, friends, co-workers or pets, can be the best champions for your venture.

❑ Take what sounds like sage advice with a grain of salt; sometimes the advice is clouded with bias, envy or knowledge from a different time.

❑ Follow your gut instinct above all.

❑ Understand that mentors may not be the best champions, especially if they too feel vulnerable in the achievement of their own goals.

❑ If your belief in your idea is strong enough, it will naturally override any feelings of self-doubt, whether self-imposed or imposed on you from others.

THE AGONY OF "NO"

As an entrepreneur, you may feel like a magnet sometimes. All kinds of interesting opportunities may present themselves to you, many unpaid. I'm thinking of sitting on boards of directors, or volunteering your time for a good cause, or committee work at your organization, or networking events, speaking opportunities, writing opportunities, mentoring opportunities, and the list can go on.

Commitment to your goal, however, sometimes requires you to say "no" to some of these opportunities. It can be really hard to do, though, especially, if you are like me, you feel flattered whenever someone asks you to help them. This is what I mean by the "agony of 'no.'" For me, saying "no" is one of the most difficult words to say. I see both good and bad with being involved in so many things. But, your plate can get too full, making your performance and mental health suffer.

If you are strong enough to say "no" when first asked, as opposed to saying "no" after you start a new obligation, you are ahead of the game. By waiting until after you start only to realize saying "yes" was a mistake, the word "no" becomes much more agonizing. So, one trait to work on if you are not already good at it, is setting boundaries by saying "no" to obligations that will only get in the way of you achieving your ambitious goal. In this context, learning to get comfortable with "no" can be quite empowering.

There is another side to the agony of "no," which is when someone else tells you "no" to something you need to move your idea forward (see Chapter 5 on Funding, for example). In this context, you may be tempted to interpret "no" as failure. But "no" is part of the process, and it is a test of your commitment to your idea or goal. If you prepare yourself for the word "no" and view it as an inevitable word in your quest to succeed, the word loses its sting. *You are not alone in being told "no."* That is worth repeating: You are not alone in being told "no." Do not look at it as defeat, but as another step in your journey.

Chapter Three

COMMITMENT

Commitment

THE IDEA OF COMMITTING TO YOUR IDEA is really an extension of overcoming self-doubt, discussed in the previous chapter. But, commitment to your ambitions requires more than overcoming self-doubt, which is more internal work. Commitment requires action. It also requires confronting the word "no" (see opposite).

Commitment is the point at which your idea permeates out of your head and becomes real. But, there are two caveats about commitment.

Caveat #1: You Don't Have to Quit Your Day Job
(at least not all of them)

Commitment does not necessarily mean you need to quit your day job, if you have one. Some entrepreneurs I've talked to state that like me, they have numerous "day jobs." When I created Pursesuitz, I had three day jobs. Trying to stay on top of three different jobs while also launching a new business is at best crazy, and at worst, deeply frustrating. Nevertheless, like many entrepreneurs who have day jobs, cutting that cord is scary, especially if you like that cord! And for me, I really liked all three of my jobs. But at some point, to make room for my new venture, something had to give. I had to do a cost-benefit analysis for each job and decide if any of the costs were greater than the benefits of my keeping that particular job. Freeing up some time so I could devote more to the success of my new venture was necessary, while still keeping some of my safety net jobs until my new one took off.

According to management researchers Joseph Rafiee and Jie Feng, who tracked 5000 would-be entrepreneurs from 1994 to 2008, those who kept their day jobs were 33 percent less likely to fail in their new venture.

That's a persuasive statistic, given that just 56% of start-ups survive to their fourth year. That means almost half of all start-ups fail after four years in. If you have a day job, then you can mitigate the risk of failure by sticking with (at least one) of your day jobs for as long as possible. This leads to the second caveat about commitment.

Caveat #2: Be Patient

Commitment also doesn't mean your idea will come to fruition quickly. As the statistics above demonstrate, a lot of entrepreneurs give up after a few years. According to one business blogger, here are five reasons why entrepreneurs give up:

1) Their purpose isn't strong enough. I would rephrase this to say that they don't truly believe in their idea. See Chapter One.

2) They have an unsupportive environment. See Chapter Two.

3) There isn't enough money to implement the idea. See the section on Funding later in this chapter.

4) They encounter lengthy delays to idea implementation. This is why this chapter starts with advising you not to quit your day job and to be patient. As the blogger states: "If your purpose is bulletproof, you'll realize that delays are part of the process."

5) Their idea fails. Well, maybe the first iteration fails, but that doesn't mean future iterations will fail. Again, if you truly believe in your idea, you will find lessons in the failure and make improvements. This is where I like to remember that twelve publishers rejected JK Rowling's *Harry Potter* book before one decided it was worth publishing. Take rejection as a badge of honor.

Knowing the reasons why so many entrepreneurs give up can arm you to fight the urge to give up. If your purpose isn't strong enough, maybe you can revise it (see Chapter Twelve on scaling back). Find your champions. Research funding options (I've done some of that for you in Chapter Five). Be patient and learn from your mistakes. Some of the most successful businesses took years to take off. The founder of Nike spent five years selling athletic shoes as a side gig while working full-time as an accountant. Sara Blakely, the founder of Spanx, kept her full-time job selling fax machines for several years before going all-in on her company. The developer of Minecraft, a popular video game, kept his day job for a full year before committing to Minecraft full-time.

That said, commitment does require you to take steps toward reaching your goal, even small ones. During the launch of Pursesuitz, I have kept my full-time job as a university professor, as well as my law firm. The income helps me pay the bills and fund the small steps I am taking for Pursesuitz. These small steps include building a prototype, registering my business with my State Department of Financial Institutions and the Internal Revenue Service, buying domain names and creating a website, filing trademark and patent applications, writing blogs, creating social media accounts, creating logos, drafting a business plan and solid sales pitch, joining business start-up groups, and researching the market. These are all things I can do on a relatively low budget in my spare time.

You might ask, *what spare time?* It's true I have two other jobs, a family and myself to take care of. And I'll admit that I am dog-tired at the end of each day. But, I find the time and energy by not participating in a lot of activities that others find time to enjoy, such as watching TV, going out on the town, or going out of town on weekends. That is my sacrifice, and as a result, to outsiders looking in my life looks quite boring. But I am not bored. Far from it. I find the work I am doing with Pursesuitz, my law firm, and Lemonspark very satisfying and really interesting. And that is what matters. As the captain of my own entrepreneurial ship, I get to decide what fulfills me, and what does not.

What if I Don't have a Day Job, or
What if I Just Feel Like I Need to Quit My Day Job?

If you don't have a day job, you are in the enviable position of being able to give 100% or more of yourself to see your new venture succeed on the fast track. As mentioned above, there are advantages to having a day job. But, also as mentioned above, there are disadvantages. The biggest disadvantage is not having enough time or energy to pour into the success of your new venture. Investors may find your full commitment more appealing than if you are juggling several different responsibilities that do not have anything to do with the success of your new business. The downside to not having a day job is the stress that comes with not being sure how you will pay your bills until your new venture is self-sufficient and producing income for you. This is where financial help from family, friends, lenders, or investors comes into play. See Chapter Five for more on that.

Some of you may feel a pull toward starting your own business, but you just aren't sure what to do yet. There is something to be said for jumping in without knowing what is ahead. Sometimes it is that first, radical step that gets your creative juices flowing and starts you on the path to fulfilling your Divine Design. When people ask me how and why I started my law firm, I tell them this story:

During the last few years that I worked as a lawyer in a big law firm, I felt "the tug" telling me I wasn't doing what I was meant to do. Of course, the tug didn't bother telling me what exactly I was supposed to be doing, just that practicing law in a big firm wasn't it. The tug caused an unsettling feeling in my gut, and would often appear at random times. In fact, while still working at the big law firm, I remember one colleague asking me how I was doing. I responded with the typical, "Fine." But he pressed me, "No, I mean how are you doing, really?" Stunned, I responded "fine" again. He pressed me again: "No, really, how are you?"

I took the bait on the third ask. "Truthfully, I feel like I am meant to do something else, but I don't know what that is." My colleague then responded with the most anti-climactic "Oh, ok." I couldn't figure out why he even bothered pressing me to answer if he wasn't going to offer me some sage, profound advice. But, what I didn't realize was that speaking out loud about that internal struggle was the first step in my doing something about it.

Fast forward four years. I made partner at my law firm and the tug didn't disappear. Then, I was recruited to work as an in-house lawyer. I thought maybe that was what I was meant to do, but the tug didn't disappear. Then, six months into my in-house job, one of my former clients called me and asked whether I would come back to private practice. He said their legal services were just not the same without me.

At that very moment, an idea popped into my head that surprised even me. The idea was to start my own law firm. An idea that was never on my bucket list. I spoke the idea out loud to my former client and he immediately agreed that it was a great idea and assured me his organization would hire me as their legal counsel.

After that meeting, the idea would not leave my head. Wise friends tried talking me out of it, for very good reasons. First, I was only six months into a new job and I should give it more time. It was a good job that offered security and interesting work. So, why leave? Second, I didn't have any real savings for a financial safety net in case my idea didn't work or at the very least took a while to take off. Third, starting a law firm is hard and I didn't really have that much experience in the administrative operations of a law firm.

Those were all sensible, logical reasons to put my idea on hold. But that tug was starting to pull harder, telling me that this might be the window of opportunity I was waiting for. And if I didn't act now, I might never know the outcome. The prospect of regret outweighed all of the sensible advice from my friends. I knew in my gut that this was a now-or- never moment, so I took it. Years later, my law firm is going strong, and I still have so many other ideas, like Pursesuitz and Lemonspark. The best part? I am no longer haunted by wondering what I am meant to do.

I tell this story as an illustration of the very real possibility that once you take that first step, you put destiny in motion. Whether that first step is simply talking about your idea, or expressing your dissatisfaction with your current state of affairs, or quitting your day job in pursuit of something more fulfilling, you start the search process. Your antennas go up and you are more receptive to the universe pointing the way. It is a liberating and enlightening process. So if you feel that tug, even if it doesn't make sense, sometimes doing the crazy thing is the best thing you can do.

Research shows that verbalizing your crazy idea is one of the best things you can do to move it forward, as discussed next.

What Steps Can Entrepreneurs Take to Stay Committed?

In their fascinating study about the early stages of entrepreneurship, researchers Victor Bennett and Aaron Chatterji of Duke University identified steps people can take to move their idea forward.[3] They asked 447 would-be entrepreneurs which of these steps did they last take before calling it quits. The results are shown opposite in Table 3.1.

I love several things about this data. First, it creates a wonderful checklist of things you can do to stay committed to your idea. Second, it reveals the various stages at which entrepreneurs give up on their commitment. They try some things and then give up, perhaps because they didn't like the feedback or the step didn't go as expected or planned.

Indeed, as shown in Table 3.1, most people's last step was discussing their idea with a friend, colleague or acquaintance. Based on the feedback from their friend, colleague or acquaintance, the most common reasons the would-be entrepreneur gave up was because they decided their idea wouldn't be profitable enough or it would be too difficult to get financing. Other reasons provided included that the competition would make their idea unprofitable, they didn't have the skills to move forward, their idea was too risky, or they were not able to complete the next step.

---

[3] Victor M. Bennett & Aaron K. Chatterji, The Entrepreneurial Process: Evidence from a Nationally Representative Survey, Duke University Press (Aug. 11, 2017), available at https://sites.duke.edu/ronniechatterji/files/2017/08/10_TheEntrepreneurialProcess_BennettChatterji_UpdatedAugust11th2017.pdf (last visited October 3, 2020).

Table 3.1
Last Step Taken Before Entrepreneurs Quit Their Idea

Last Step Taken	Number Who Quit After That Last Step
Discussed idea with a friend, work colleague or acquaintance	170
Searched the Internet or stores to explore whether an existing organization already provided the service or product your business would produce	59
Consulted a friend or acquaintance who was an expert on your target market	25
Sought out someone you did not already know who was an expert on your target market and discussed the idea with them.	14
Created some sort of document (power point presentation, executive summary, etc.)	8
Created spreadsheets, financial models, or other numerical analysis to determine feasibility	14
Wrote a business plan	23
Made a sale	36
Built a working prototype or provided the service on a pilot basis	13
Tested demand for your product or service (i.e., surveys or advertising the business, whether up-and-running or not)	8
Approached a lawyer or accountant or researched the legal or tax implications of starting the business	14
Built a website for the business	13
Collected feedback from customers who used your product	8
Applied to an incubator/accelerator program or business plan competition	0
Explored financing options with a bank, investors or grant program	27
Explored using patents, copyright, or trademark to protect your business idea	3
Used feedback from pilot or demand testing to change business idea	2
Explicitly considered how other firms might respond if you launched the business	10

Source: Bennett & Chatterji, The Entrepreneurial Process (see footnote opposite)

It's important to remember, however, the motivations behind your friends, colleagues, and acquaintances. As I state in Chapter Two, many times would-be mentors are clouded with jealousy or competition and they may not have your best interest in mind. In fact, they may try to sabotage your idea, just like my mentor did when I tried to become partner. Talking to others is a great step, but you must take their feedback with knowledge and caution.

What surprised Bennett and Chatterji was how few steps most would-be entrepreneurs took to move their idea forward. They found that more than 80 percent of those considering entrepreneurship had never spoken to someone they did not already know about their business idea! This is a very low-cost, easy step that the vast majority of would-be entrepreneurs are unwilling to take.

So, when you feel your commitment to your idea wane, talk to someone about your idea, especially a stranger who would be in your target market. That's what I did when I spoke to my dear friend Rhonda. Upon hearing my idea, she encouraged me to keep going, even if at a slower pace. The very act of talking to someone will already put you far out front of most would-be entrepreneurs. If you don't like what you hear from strangers, don't despair. Learn from them and improve your idea based on their feedback, like I did with my focus groups. This is called market research and I believe every new business needs to do it, which we discuss in Chapter Six.

What If I Lose Steam?

It's ok. You know what? If you take as many steps as you can only to lose interest in your idea, you no longer have to wonder "What if?" To me, not knowing what could have been is one of life's most tragic circumstances. To the extent you have the ability to avoid wondering "What if?," take advantage of that opportunity. Sometimes we can't control the "What if's" in life, but the ones we can, we should. If you can go far enough down a road to know that going any further will not bring you joy or fulfillment, then I call that success. You paid attention to your tug and it taught you something. With that knowledge, the tug will lead you to your next opportunity. That is what happened with Pursesuitz. I followed my tug, created the first prototype, then received unexpected and critical feedback. I then scaled back (see Chapter Twelve) to fit the market demand. Upon seeing the revised prototype, incorporating the feedback from the focus groups, I was so delighted with the outcome. My faith in Pursesuitz was renewed.

But you know what else happened during the months I questioned my belief in Pursesuitz? My earlier idea involving Lemonspark crept back into my life. I had put Lemonspark on hold for over a decade. Not because I thought it was a bad idea, but because life became too busy. Through working with my law firm clients, I learned about the possibilities of podcasts and online educational resources and retreats. In my head, I started to apply these ideas to Lemonspark and soon found myself with a renewed energy to revive Lemonspark as a podcast, which I did.

Just like Pursesuitz, though, it doesn't matter if Lemonspark goes viral. What matters is if it helps at least one person who is facing a traumatic time in his or her life and finds hope, inspiration, and a sense of belonging. Keeping that in mind makes doing the podcast so rewarding. I am convinced that had I not started down the Pursesuitz road, Lemonspark would still be on my backburner. Pursesuitz opened my eyes to other worthwhile endeavors, and there is significant value in that.

Keep Talking

One of the best ways to stay committed to your idea is to keep talking about it with people. Talking about your idea with new people expands your network.

If networking with others causes you anxiety or depletes your energy, you may be an introvert. And you are in good company. According to Jon Levy of *Forbes Magazine*, one-third to one-half of all people are introverts. But it is still possible to network as an introvert. It may take more courage than an extrovert, but once you learn the formula for networking, it gets easier.

First, networking is not sales. Networking is really market research. A lot of introverts can appreciate research, so if you think of networking as researching the current status of the market in which you work, networking becomes a very interesting task.

So, when approaching people you don't know, as a market researcher, you want to find out about who they are, as well as what interests or excites them. Here is an exercise to try with a complete stranger in a professional setting:

Exercise: Networking with Strangers

If you find yourself at a networking event, such as a fundraiser, client development event, or evening reception, develop some market research questions in advance. Some potential questions might be:

❑ I am thinking about developing this idea (then describe the idea). Would this be something that might interest you or someone you know? If not, why not?

❑ If it does interest you, how much would you be willing to pay for it?

❑ I am aiming to write an article about what keeps individuals in this industry up at night. What are some things that concern you?

❑ I am looking to write a career development book for individuals starting out in my profession. What advice would you give to those just breaking into this market?

❑ I am doing a survey of the volunteer opportunities in the community and wondering what opportunities you take advantage of or are aware of? I hope to put the answers into a publication that will raise awareness of individuals in my field of the ways in which they can contribute to our communities.

Commitment

You can probably think of additional questions to ask; these are just to get you started. Then, when you find yourself at the event, have a notepad with you and try the following steps:

❏ Walk up to someone who is alone or not in the midst of a conversation;

❏ Introduce yourself with a smile and extended or waving hand;

❏ After the person returns the introduction, ask them if they would mind if you asked them some questions about a research project on which you are working.

❏ They may ask you to provide further details about your research project, to which you respond that you are conducting some market research for your business and would really like to get feedback from as many unique perspectives as possible.

❏ Assuming they say yes, (I can't imagine anyone turning down a friendly request to answer some questions), ask them your questions and take notes on your notepad. Nothing looks more legitimate that you are actually conducting research if you write down what the interviewee is saying.

❏ Assuming you are listening to what they are telling you, you will likely have follow up questions, like asking them to explain something a bit more. When relevant and appropriate, weave in your own expertise, experience and interests to the conversation. If you are hoping the conversation might lead to opportunities for you, ask the person for their business card and suggest that you would like to follow up with them to continue the conversation.

❏ It is better to collect more business cards than you give out. Possessing a business card puts you in the driver's seat as to when and how you follow up with the contact. If all you do is give out your business card without collecting any from others, you will need to wait, and hope, that they contact you. In my experience, very few people contact you after collecting your business card.

This market research can actually lead to work product, such as an article, blog or even book. One of the best ways to capitalize on your efforts from your day job is to use the information you learn to write an article or create a presentation about what you learned. Better yet, do both! I am a big believer on repurposing as much material as possible. It is that extra step that will get you noticed by those who have the ability to promote you.

Interestingly, the research by Bennett and Chatterji revealed that we are much more willing to take steps in advancing our career on the job market than we are in advancing an entrepreneurial idea. Unemployed as well as employed workers were more likely to reach out to people they did not already know when job searching. For example, 65 percent of unemployed workers were willing to contact employers directly, while 42 percent of employed workers reached out to employers directly. Yet, only 20 percent of potential entrepreneurs spoke about their business idea to someone they did not already know.

The researchers could not explain the difference between one's willingness to reach out to strangers when searching for jobs and less willingness to do so when exploring an entrepreneurial idea. But, based on the Bennett and Chatterji's study, we know that talking about your idea to others helps in staying committed to the idea. So, if you are a would-be entrepreneur, be part of the minority and start talking!

Have Faith

According to one of my favorite authors, Florence Scovel Shinn, "Fear is misdirected energy and must be redirected, or transmuted into Faith." (Scovel Shinn, p. 53) In answer to the question of how to overcome fear, Ms. Scovel Shinn instructs us to walk up to the thing of which we are afraid. Only by doing the thing we fear will we become the people we are meant to be. Ms. Scovel Shinn was one of the earliest "wellness professionals" in the early 20th century. She was widely known as an artist and illustrator, metaphysician, and lecturer, having helped thousands of people through her work of healing and solving their problems.

It is so important to not let fear hold you back from achieving your goal. As an entrepreneur, you owe it to yourself to be courageous and have faith in your abilities.

Commitment

Once you commit to your idea, you must continually have faith in it. Part of fostering that faith is to envision your future and how your idea plays out as you move through each step. Ms. Scovel Shinn subscribes to the idea of continually "making believe" that you are already successful. By acting as though your idea is already successful, it has a better chance of actually coming true. Your "body and affairs show forth what [you] have been picturing." (Scovel Shinn, p. 30-31). "The sick man has pictured sickness, the poor man, poverty, the rich man, wealth."

This is good advice for me at the moment. As I write this, the Coronavirus of 2019 or "COVID 19" has shut down much of the United States. My kids are home from school. University students are finishing the Spring 2020 semester by taking all classes online. Graduations and proms are canceled. Movie theaters, bars and restaurants are closed. Life has changed completely in the course of one week.

These changes certainly disrupt my plan for Pursesuitz. The changes cause me to wonder how important will purse-free blouses be to women in the wake of all this chaos? But, keeping the faith means not wavering, even with COVID 19. Perhaps it means adjusting my timeline or my product goals, but it doesn't mean scrapping my idea. There is a

---

PURSESUITZ SIDENOTE

After I conducted the focus groups in Spring/Summer of 2020, I learned that my intended audience—professional women—were more interested in my product for travel or leisure purposes. They didn't like the top "professional" layer. And, the gender equality messaging that I thought was so powerful didn't resonate with them. I thought professional women would be drawn to professional clothing that included functional pockets to put them on more equal footing with men's professional clothes, which has plenty of functional pockets. To my surprise, the focus group women didn't understand the connection between gender equality and Pursesuitz

(continued on p. 42)

(continued from p. 41)

Clothing. There was too much explaining required to bridge the gap between having functional pockets and achieving gender equality. The focus group women were much more interested in the product and the fact that it had functional pockets than with the whole idea of achieving gender equality with the product.

Furthermore, with so many people now working remotely, there was less interest and need for professional clothes. After much painful internal deliberation, I decided to focus on the inner layer only. I also decided to focus the messaging on the pockets, not gender equality. This meant I had to re-order my labels and re-do my website, which had stated as the tag line "Pursuing Gender Equality with Style."

Instead, I concluded a more meaningful description of my hero product was that it functioned as "Pocketwear." Pocketwear was a new term to me, and I thought of it as I discussed with my husband how I would categorize the revised inner layer. Was it athleisure-wear or was it underwear? Technically it could function as either, and I didn't want a category or label to limit the possibilities the revised product provided. So, I thought of the term "Pocketwear" and decided to trademark it.

termination date for everything, even COVID 19. My commitment to my idea does not have to weaken because of external chaos. It may evolve to fit circumstances, but it can still serve a purpose. See Pursesuitz Sidenote for an example of how COVID-19 changed Pursesuitz.

According to Ms. Scovel Shinn, faith is nonresistance. In other words, having faith means not being affected by stormy situations. When pursuing your ambition, things will not always go as planned. There will be hiccups and disruptions. But stay the course. Do not overreact or give into fear that the hiccup means failure. When you are truly faithful to your idea, you cannot be touched or influenced by the negative thoughts of others or by negative situations. (Scovel Shinn, p. 31). If you agree that the adverse situation is good and are undisturbed by it, it will fall away of its own weight. (Scovel Shinn, p. 34).

Affirm your faith in the face of adversity by saying "None of these things move me." Those are powerful words. And then, through all the storms in which you have remained steadfast to your idea, your ship will come in. "One's ships come in over a calm sea." (Scovel Shinn, p. 34). Your ability to stay calm internally while the external world rolls through chaos will one day make your dreams come true. Perhaps even better than you expected.

CHECKLIST FOR COMMITMENT

❏ Be patient. If possible, stay at your day job while you pursue your idea.

❏ Talk about your idea, particularly with people you don't know. It helps cement your commitment.

❏ Write your business plan. It helps you create the vision for your future.

❏ Do the things you fear the most. It is the only way to become who you are meant to be.

❏ Replace fear with faith. Remain steadfast in your idea, even through stormy seas.

CHAPTER 4

THE LEGAL STUFF

I AM A LAWYER BY TRADE, SO I FEEL obligated to write about the legal side to starting a new venture (if you are reading this book for career advancement within a company, go ahead and skip this chapter). In all honesty, it is probably the least fun aspect of starting a new business, but a necessary one. Some questions that arise in the legal arena to start-ups are:

1. What type of legal entity should I choose, if any?

2. Can I change my legal entity type later?

3. How do I form such a legal entity?

4. How do I get a tax ID number?

5. What types of insurance should I have?

6. How and when should protect any intellectual property (and what is "intellectual property" anyway)?

7. Should I hire a lawyer?

8. What, if any, regulatory compliance issues should concern me? (Later in the book is a special section devoted to health and wellness start-ups.)

What Type of Legal Entity Should I choose, if Any?

Many new entrepreneurs wrestle with the decision of whether to create a legal entity at all. I have had many clients ask me should I even bother? The basis for this question is that when you venture out on your own, you become a "sole proprietor" unless you actively register your business with a State, such as your own state or another state like Delaware. So, the default legal status of any new business is sole proprietor, or partnership if you decide to enter a partnership agreement with someone.

The pros and cons of creating a legal entity or just using the default "sole proprietor" status are as follows:

Table 4.1
Pros and Cons of Having Legal Status of Sole Proprietorship[4]

Pros	Cons
No required state paperwork for the business[5]	You can be sued personally for your business activities, putting your personal assets at risk
No annual state filings[6]	Investors don't like investing in sole proprietorships
Profits/losses pass through to owner's personal tax return (therefore no business or unemployment taxes)	It's hard to obtain business loans and credit; instead you may get and use "personal loans" or credit.
Can deduct use of personal items for business purposes from personal income tax, as well as other business expenses	You may have lower market credibility because you do not operate under a trade name (but you can register a "Doing Business As" name with your state department of revenue or Secretary of State, which requires initial and ongoing fees).

As you can surmise from Table 4.1, most sole proprietors use their own name as the name of their business. You don't have to, but then you must register your "Doing Business As" ("DBA") name with the state, which defeats one of the benefits of sole proprietorships (not having to file anything with the State).

If using your own name as your business or exposing your personal assets to potential risk does not appeal to you, then creating a separate legal entity is probably a good idea. If you decide to create a separate

---

4 These pros and cons are courtesy of John Tucker, LLC v. Sole Proprietor: How to Make the Right Choice for Your Business (Dec. 3, 2019), available at https://www.nav.com/blog/llc-sole-proprietor-18376/#:~:text=One%20of%20the%20key%20benefits,debts%20incurred%20by%20the%20business. (last visited June 14, 2020).

5 This assumes the business owner doesn't need any industry-specific licenses, such as a law or healthcare license, in which case the owner would need to complete that paperwork.

6 See above footnote.

legal entity, then you must choose which type of legal entity. There are several from which to choose. The most common types are C Corporations, S Corporations, and Limited Liability Corporations. Here is a chart comparing the pros and cons of incorporating into one of these legal entities compared with using a sole proprietorship.

Table 4.2
Pros and Cons of Incorporating Your Business (as Opposed to Having a Sole Proprietorship)[7]

Pros	Cons
More market credibility	Must file initial documents with the State to register
You are not personally liable for debts or lawsuits against the company	Must file annual documents and pay annual fees
Easier to get financing from lenders and investors	May pay more in taxes (such as business and unemployment taxes)
If you elect LLC status, you can be taxed as a sole proprietor and can deduct business expenses from your individual tax return	Tax return fees may be higher than completing an individual tax return

Limited Liability Companies (LLCs)

LLCs are a popular option for incorporation because they offer a lot of flexibility and do not require a board of directors, annual meetings, or other formalities, for example (which is the case for C corporations). As an LLC, you can choose to be taxed as a corporation, a partnership, or as a disregarded entity.[8] Multi-member LLCs (more than one owner) are taxed as partnerships by default, unless the owners elect a different status. Single member LLCs are taxed as disregarded entities by default, unless a different election is made. For both partnerships and disregarded entities, any income made by the business is passed through to the owners and taxed as personal income. In other words, the company itself is not taxed; only the owners. For some, this is an attractive option

---

[7] These pros and cons are courtesy of John Tucker, LLC v. Sole Proprietor: How to Make the Right Choice for Your Business (Dec. 3, 2019), available at https://www.nav.com/blog/llc-sole-proprietor-18376 (last visited June 14, 2020).

[8] From Lexis Practical Advisor, Incorporation Considerations for Start-Ups (June 2020).

because it can avoid double taxation: if you make money at your business and your business status is a C corporation, for example, the business is taxed and any income you make as the owner in wages, for example, is also taxed as personal income.

C Corporations

If you want to raise venture capital for your business, then C corporation status is likely the way to go. Why? One reason is that C corporations can offer stock (and different types of stock, such as common stock or preferred stock). Investors want to minimize their tax burden, and with C corporations, they can receive investment returns in the form of capital appreciation, which is subject to the much lower capital gains tax rate. If investors receive dividends or other income, however, that is taxed at the much higher personal income tax rate. The different classes of stock that a C corporation can offer allows owners and investors flexibility to determine how much voting power is assigned to each class of stock, and give priority to certain classes over others when it comes to financial distributions. Founders of C corporations can create more control over their company by limiting certain classes of stock to founders only, and giving those classes super-voting rights to maintain more control over the company.[9]

Another reason venture capitalists prefer C corporations over other types of legal entities is that there are no restrictions in who can invest in the corporation. Many times, venture capital funds consist of different legal entities, such as trusts, other corporations, or foreign entities. Other legal entity types, such as S corporations, may restrict who can invest in and own part of that corporation. Thus, C corporations provide flexibility in terms of who or what can invest in the company to help it grow. But, as mentioned above, one of the downsides to C corporation status is that the corporation is taxed on any income it generates, as well as the owners

---

[9] See Upcounsel, Classes of Stock: Everything You Need to Know, available at https://www.upcounsel.com/classes-of-stock (last visited June 20, 2020)

to the extent they earn any income from the corporation (such as wages or salaries). So, unlike a pass-through entity, such as a sole proprietorship or LLC, owners of a C corporation may be taxed twice.

S Corporations

S Corporations are not as flexible from an investment standpoint as C corporations. There is only one class of stock, but you can still have stock with voting rights and without voting rights, even though they are in the same class.[10] However, the real downside to S corporations for some start-ups is with who can invest in S corporations. S corporations limit investors to U.S. individuals, estates, and certain trusts. Corporations, partnerships and foreign entities are not permitted to invest in S corporations. This can limit the number and type of investors from which a start-up can seek help to grow. Also, S corporations can have no more than 100 shareholders, which if you envision your company ever being traded publicly one day, S-corporation status will not work.

Nevertheless, S-corporation status can be advantageous from a tax perspective for the owner. An LLC can elect S corporation status. Like sole proprietors and partnerships, S corporations are taxed at the owner level. As a result, the corporation itself is not taxed. Instead, all shareholders are taxed individually on their personal income tax return for their share of income, as well as possibly deduct from their personal passive income their share of losses from the corporation.

Another advantage of an S corporation, and why many start-ups choose this option, is for tax advantages that occur when the owner also treats herself as an employee of the company. If an S corporation owner treats herself as an employee and receives a W-2 from the company from which social security and unemployment taxes are deducted, any amount the company earns above the employee compensation amount is exempt from social security and unemployment taxes.

---

[10] From LexisNexis Practical Advisor, Pass-Through Entities Taxation (June 2020).

Let's look at an example of how this might offer tax savings. Let's say you start a business, choose an LLC and to be taxed as an S corporation. You decide to pay yourself wages of $30,000 per year. Using current tax rates for both the employer and employee share of social security and unemployment taxes (also called FICA and FUTA), which is about 21.3%, you would pay $6,390 in taxes.

Salary: $30,000
FICA/FUTA deduction (employer and employee share): 21.3%
$30,000*21.3%=$6,390.

Now let's say your company earns $60,000 during the year. The additional $30,000 earned above your salary would not be subject to FICA and FUTA tax (but would still be subject to federal and state income tax). So, you could take a shareholder "draw" from that additional $30,000 and report it as income on your taxes, but you would not be paying another $6,390 in FICA/FUTA taxes on that shareholder draw. So, you could save yourself $6,390 in taxes by choosing the S-corporation status.

Please note that not every state or local jurisdiction recognizes S-corporation status. So, before electing this status, it is important to check whether it is available in your jurisdiction.

The following table compares the features of different types of available legal entities for start-ups.

Table 4.3
Comparing the Different Legal Entities*

CONCERN	GENERAL PARTNERSHIP	LIMITED PARTNERSHIP	LLC	CORPORATION (SOMETIMES CALLED A C-CORP.)	S-CORPORATION
Limited Liability? (liability limited to the amount of investment)	NO	YES for limited partner NO for general partner	YES	YES	YES
Pass through taxation? (taxation passes through the entity to the individuals)	YES	YES	YES (can elect other forms of taxation)	NO ("double taxation" both corporation and shareholders pay taxes)	YES (note- still need to file a corporate tax return)
Continuous life or tenuous?	Tenuous (absent agreement to the contrary) Possibility of dissolution by any partner withdrawing	Somewhat tenuous (absent agreement to the contrary) Limited partner leaving is not dissolution but a general partner leaving will cause dissolution	Very stable (duration as stated in the agreement)	Very stable (stockholders may come and go with little effect)	Very stable (stockholders may come and go with little effect)
Management & authority to control affairs	Shared equally by all partners	Centralized in the general partners	Flexible – either shared or centralized; managed by members (member managed) or by managers (manager managed)	Centralized in the board of directors	Centralized in the board of directors
Number of "persons" needed to form" (person can be natural or fictional)	2 or more	2 or more (1 Limited Partner and 1 General Partner)	1 or more	1 or more	1 or more; see limits on owners
Formalities & fees for formation?	Informal Usually no filing or fees required to set up and manage	More formal than general partnership, less than other entities Limited filings and fees	Formal requirements for filing and fees Less formalities to observe after formation (as compared to a corporation) but more than a general partnership or limited partnership	Formal requirements for filing and fees Corporate formalities must be strictly observed (maintenance of separate books, records, and accounts; completion of various filings; periodic meetings or written consents of directors and shareholders)	Formal requirements for filing and fees plus additional IRS election (form 2553) Corporate formalities must be strictly observed (maintenance of separate books, records, and accounts; completion of various filings; periodic meetings or written consents of directors and shareholders)

[6] From LexisNexis Practical Advisor (May 31, 2020).

(Continued on page 52)

(*Continued from page 51*)

CONCERN	GENERAL PARTNERSHIP	LIMITED PARTNERSHIP	LLC	CORPORATION (SOMETIMES CALLED A C-CORP.)	S-CORPORATION.
Interest transferred to 3rd parties?	**Limited transferability** One cannot transfer entire interest, absent agreement to the contrary; share of profits can be transferred	**Limited transferability** Partners have more flexibility in transferring their interest in capital and assets are assignable, but cannot assign reserved interest in control	**Restricted transferability** In most jurisdictions, transferability restrictions on ownership interest Will often depend on buy/sell provisions in the operating agreement and state law	**Freely transferable** Absent agreement to the contrary, freely transferable among shareholders	**Freely transferable** Free transferability but there are **restrictions** on the type and number of shareholders (corporations, trusts and nonresident aliens may not be shareholders)

Can I Change My Legal Entity Type Later?

Yes, you can change an LLC or partnership to a C corporation if you decide later that you would like to be more attractive to outside investors. How much work this conversion entails depends on your state's laws (i.e., the state in which your start-up was formed and the states in which the start-up is qualified to do business). If your state allows statutory conversion, the process is much simpler than if your state does not allow it. According to one source, most states allow statutory conversions, but 15 states do not.[11] You can find out what your state allows by visiting this website: https://www.nolo.com/legal-encyclopedia/50-state-guide-converting-llc-corporation.html.

Statutory conversions involve filing specific forms with the appropriate secretaries of state, as well as creating a conversion plan that must be approved by all LLC members or all partners in the partnership.[12] Once all the forms are filed and created, however, the conversion is automatic. LLC members become stockholders of the new corporation and all debts and assets are now debts and assets of the new corporation.

---

[11] David Steingold, Converting an LLC to a Corporation in Illinois, Nolo available at https://www.nolo.com/legal-encyclopedia/converting-llc-corporation-illinois.html (last visited June 20, 2020).

[12] From LexisNexis Practical Advisor, Incorporations Considerations for Start-Ups (June 2020).

If your state does not allow a statutory conversion, then you will most likely need to use the "statutory merger" process to convert your LLC or partnership into a C corporation. The statutory merger approach is much more formal and requires you to first create a new C corporation with your secretary of state and then file a certificate of merger with the secretary of state. The company owners have to vote and approve the merger both as members of the LLC (or partners of the partnership) and then as shareholders of the new C corporation. Once the merger is complete, the former LLC or partnership is dissolved by filing with the secretary of state the necessary paperwork to dissolve a business entity. In other words, the statutory merger process requires a lot more filings with the secretary of state!

Fortunately, in my home state of Wisconsin statutory conversion is available. Although I created Pursesuitz as an LLC, I am considering converting it to a C corporation so that it can be more attractive to investors. This may cost me a bit more in filing fees (because I had to pay the filing fee when I created the LLC, and will have to pay another filing fee if and when I convert to a C corporation), but it will be worth it if the conversion makes Pursesuitz more attractive to investors. This is not something I need to do immediately, however. It will depend on what types of investors may want to invest in Pursesuitz. If individuals only want to be investors, and I get the rest of the money I need through bank loans, I may not need to convert to a C corporation. However, if I desire to attract venture capital to fund my business, converting to C corporation status will likely need to occur.

All this information about conversion is meant to convey that you don't have to choose the perfect legal entity option at the start. The law permits you to change your mind once your venture is up and running. Yes, conversions may make things more expensive than if you chose the correct option at first, but it can be fixed. So, don't invest too much of your time worrying about which legal entity you should pick. But, hopefully the above discussion will help you make the right decision for you at this moment.

How Do I Form My Legal Entity?

As you may have guessed from the first part of this chapter, forming your legal entity requires filing forms with your state's secretary of state, unless you plan to be a sole proprietor, in which case you do nothing but get to work. Partnerships should have a written partnership agreement, but do not need to file anything with the secretary of state. Note: your state may not call the agency in charge of corporate filings the "secretary of state." Case in point: the agency in charge of corporate filings and records in my home state of Wisconsin is called the Department of Financial Institutions. A good resource to get you started with finding your state agency can be found at https://www.nolo.com/legal-encyclopedia/form-llc -in-your-state-31019.html. It is typical for the same state agency to be in charge of all types of corporate entities.

Exactly what documents you will need to file with the secretary of state will depend on the type of legal entity you choose. For example, forming an LLC requires filing Articles of Organization. In Wisconsin, the Articles of Organization require the following information:

- A statement that the LLC is organized under the laws of Wisconsin.

- A name for the LLC.

- The street address of the registered office and the name of the registered agent at that office.

- If management of the LLC is vested in one or more managers, a statement to that effect.

- The name and address of each person organizing the LLC.[13]

In Wisconsin, the Articles of Organization is something you fill out and submit online, so much of the required language is automatically populated in the document. The only things you are really filling out are

---

[13] Wis. Stat. s. 183.0202.

names and addresses. The "registered agent" is someone who would receive a legal document, such as a subpoena or court order. Usually, for start-ups, that can be the owner of the company. Bigger companies may assign registered agent status to a company specializing in such services.

As far as whether the LLC is managed by members or managers, that is something you must decide up front, but note that you can amend your articles of organization later if you change your mind. An LLC that is managed by members means that everyone who becomes a member of the LLC will have a say in how the company is run. So, if individuals invest in your LLC, they become a member with a certain number of "units" and will be able to vote on important issues about operating the company. If the LLC is managed by "managers," then the LLC will have a management committee or board that will be able to vote on certain issues, without input from all the members. In a way, then, creating an LLC that is managed by managers is akin to having different classes of stock in a corporation: a manager-managed LLC gives managers more power than a mere member.

Although it is not filed with the secretary of state, an LLC will also need an operating agreement once there is more than one member of the LLC. The operating agreement spells out who votes on what and when, how additional members are allowed to join the LLC, compensation issues, and other important matters. This is where having legal counsel will be very helpful.

How Do I Get a Tax ID Number?

You should apply for a tax identification number for your business (or Employer Identification Number or EIN) through the Internal Revenue Service (IRS) website at https://www.irs.gov/businesses/small-businesses-self-employed/apply-for-an-employer-identification-number-ein-online.

Be careful that you are actually on the IRS website and not some other knock-off site. There are companies out there who try to scam you into thinking you can apply for an EIN through them, but if you fall for that ploy, it will end up costing you more, or even worse, not lead to an EIN at all.

If you are a sole proprietor or partnership, you will be filing taxes using your social security number or some other personal taxpayer identification number. So, you don't need to apply for a separate tax ID.

What Types of Insurance Should I Have?

If you plan to provide services for your venture, especially if you need a license to provide such services, you should have professional liability insurance (sometimes known as "errors and omissions" insurance). Beyond that, you should purchase general liability insurance to cover any bodily injury or property damages your products or services may cause.

Make sure the building in which you operate your business, whether through building ownership or rent (this could be your home or a commercial space) has property insurance. This insurance protects the building and contents of the building from vandalism, theft, fire and other types of damage.

Some insurers offer a business owner's policy, which combines the different types of insurance a small business owner needs into one package. This may be business interruption insurance, property insurance, vehicle coverage, liability insurance and crime insurance.[14] Check with your insurance agent to find out if this is an option.

Once you hire employees, you will need worker's compensation insurance, which covers expenses relating to employees who are injured on the job.

If you have a C corporation with a board of directors, you will want Directors and Officers insurance, which protects board members from the expenses of a lawsuit should the company get sued.

---

[14] From *Forbes*, 13 Types of Insurance a Small Business Owner Should Have (Jan. 19, 2012), available at https://www.forbes.com/sites/thesba/2012/01/19/13-types-of-insurance-a-small-business-owner-should-have/#9c3df0720d39 (last visited June 20, 2020).

Finally, business owners should consider cyberliability insurance, especially if the business will be collecting, storing or transmitting sensitive data. In the event of a data breach, cyberliability insurance will help pay for expenses in responding to the breach, which can be very high. As a lawyer, I have helped numerous healthcare clients work through data breaches and the expenses can easily climb into the hundreds of thousands of dollars. Cyberliabilty insurance has saved these businesses from bankruptcy.

How and When Should I Protect Any Intellectual Property (and what is "intellectual property" anyway)?

According to the Legal Information Institute at Cornell Law School, intellectual property is "any product of the human intellect that the law protects from unauthorized use by others. The ownership of intellectual property inherently creates a limited monopoly in the protected property." [15]

There are several types of intellectual property: trademarks, patents and copyright. It is important to know which intellectual property concept protects which unique creation so that you seek the correct type of protection. See Table 4.4 on page 58. It is also a good idea to hire an intellectual property lawyer to assist in seeking such protection.

Trademarks and Service Marks

Trademarks protect words or symbols that identify goods, and service marks protect words or symbols that identify services, but people often use the term "trademark" in reference to both goods and services. Entrepreneurs may use trademarks to protect the name, slogan and/or logo of their products or programs they create.

As long as the trademark is used in commerce (i.e., for business purposes), it has common law protection. This means that if someone

---

[15] Cornell Law School Legal Information Institute, Intellectual Property, available at https://www.law.cornell.edu/wex/intellectual_property (last visited June 20, 2020).

Table 4.4
Types of Protection for Various Creations

Creation Type	Copy-right	Trade-mark	Service Mark	Patent	State Business Registration Department	Website Domain Name	Trade Secret
Business Name					X	X	
Invention (new technology or tool)				X			X
Business Slogan			X				
Product Slogan		X					
Business Logo			X				
Product Logo		X					
Book	X						
Music	X						
Recipe							X
Formula							X
Product Design				X			X
Pricing Schedule							X
Customer list							X
Manufacturing Technique				X			X
Marketing Strategy							X

else tries to use your trademark for a similar product or service within your geographic area, you might be able to stop them by using state unfair competition laws and the common law. Unregistered trademarks use **TM** for goods or **SM** for services, to indicate "common law" protection for the trademark or service mark.

To obtain further protection for trademarks, business owners can register the trademark or service mark with the United States Patent and Trademark Office (USPTO). Federal registration of a trademark with the USPTO provides notice to the public of the registrant's claim of ownership of the mark, a legal presumption of ownership nationwide, and the exclusive right to use the mark on or in connection with the goods or services set forth in the registration. Registered trademarks use the ® symbol for the mark.

I have applied for trademark registration with the USPTO for Pursesuitz Pocketwear, the Pursesuitz logo, Lemonspark, and the Lemonspark logo.

Patents

A patent is a limited duration property right relating to an invention, granted by the USPTO in exchange for public disclosure of the invention. Patentable materials include machines, manufactured articles, industrial processes, and chemical compositions. Patents protect the product or process between approximately 15 to 20 years, depending on whether it is a design, utility or plant patent.

For Pursesuitz, I plan to seek a design patent to protect the design of the Pocketwear tank top. A design patent protects how a product looks, not how it functions, and offers such protection for 14 years. A design patent allows you to prevent others from making, using, selling, or importing your design.[16]

To protect a product's unique function, you need to apply for a utility patent. Utility patents are more common in the marketplace than design patents. Applying for a utility patent is usually much more expensive and time-consuming process compared to the design patent application process. Utility patents can take years to obtain and cost tens of thousands of dollars before the USPTO issues the patent. By comparison, it is reasonable to expect obtaining a design patent within a few months to a year and possible to only spend less than $1000 to obtain. However, if you obtain a utility patent, you can stop others from making, using, selling and importing the invention for 20 years, instead of the 14-year timeframe for design patents.

Trade Secret

---

[16] See USPTO at https://www.uspto.gov/web/offices/pac/mpep/s1502.html (last visited June 20, 2020); see also Richard Stim, Types of Patents under U.S. Law, Nolo, https://www.nolo.com/legal-encyclopedia/types-patents.html, available at https://www.nolo.com/legal-encyclopedia/types-patents.html (last visited on June 20, 2020).

A trade secret exists if all three of the following elements are present:

1. You have information that has economic value by virtue of it not being generally known to the public;

2. You have information that has value to others who cannot legitimately obtain the information; and

3. You have exerted reasonable effort to maintain the information's secrecy.[17]

Two well-known products with coveted trade secrets include Kentucky Fried Chicken and Coca-Cola. The recipes for those products are trade secrets and have economic value to both the companies that own them and to the consumers who wish they knew those recipes.

Unlike patents or trademarks, trade secrets are not something you register with the US Patent and Trademark Office. Rather, as the owner of a trade secret, you decide that your formula, process, or recipe is valuable and should be kept a secret. And then you actually keep it a secret. If you do that, there are state and federal laws that can help you seek a remedy should someone try to steal your trade secret. Those laws include the Economic Espionage Act of 1996 (where the federal government prosecutes theft of trade secrets) and the Defend Trade Secret Act of 2016, where you as the trade secret owner could sue someone for misappropriation of a trade secret.

Copyright

A copyright protects original works of authorship including literary, dramatic, musical, and artistic works, such as poetry, novels, movies, songs, computer software, and architecture. Copyrights can protect the original work of art for many, many years. For individual works of art (whether music or books, for example), copyright protects the work for

---

[17] US Patent Trademark Office Fact Sheet, Trade Secret Policy, available at https:/www.uspto.gov/ip-policy/trade-secret-policy (last visited February 24, 2021).

the life of the author plus 70 years. Individuals can register their copyrighted material with the U.S. Copyright Office at https://www.copyright.gov/registration/. Examples of items one can register for copyright include literary works, performing arts (music, sound recordings, scripts, stage plays), visual arts (artwork, illustrations, jewelry, fabric, architecture), computer programs, databases, blogs, websites, motion pictures and photographs.

Copyright infringement occurs when someone uses copyrighted material without permission of the author/creator. For example, to reprint information from textbooks, it is necessary to obtain permission from the publisher prior to reprinting a portion of it in another publication. Also, regarding using music for your business, it will be necessary to purchase licensing agreements from Performing Rights Organizations (PROs) such as:

- Broadcast Music, Inc. (BMI): www.bmi.com
- American Society of Composers, Authors, and Publishers (ASCAP): www.ascap.com
- Society of European Stage Authors and Composers (SECAC): www.sesac.com

Some businesses may be exempt from paying these fees based on the Fairness in Music Licensing Act (FMLA). For example, restaurants may play music from a radio using one receiver without needing a license. Other exemptions may apply. Before using music, videos, software, or other forms of creations that are copyrighted, businesses need to consult with a competent intellectual property lawyer to be sure they are not violating any copyright laws, otherwise they may face costly penalties.[18]

---

[18] See Trademark, Patent, or Copyright? U.S. Patent and Trademark Office, available at https://www.uspto.gov/trademarks-getting-started/trademark-basics/trademark-patent-or-copyright, accessed October 19, 2019; see also Registration Portal. U.S. Copyright Office, available at: https://www.copyright.gov/registration/, accessed January 12, 2020.

Should I Hire a Lawyer?

I am glad you asked! Please excuse me while I get on my soapbox for a moment. As a practicing lawyer, I cannot tell you how many times people have called or emailed me asking me for my legal advice without any intention of paying me a dime. I'm not quite sure how these folks imagine my business model, but they clearly do not understand how lawyers or law firms earn income. As with many professions, what we sell is our judgment and advice. In order to be able to offer that judgment and advice, we spend years learning our craft, just like other types of professions. So, when you contact a lawyer, please do not expect them to give you free legal advice. They may give you a free consult to see if they are a good fit for your business needs, but they should not and most likely will not be giving away their legal advice for free.

That being said, when it comes to forming and protecting your business, a good lawyer can be a very good investment. I usually tell my clients that hiring competent legal counsel for your business is like purchasing insurance for your business: both aim to protect your investment from a potential disaster.

Scattered throughout this chapter, I make reference to hiring lawyers at different times. It is probably a good idea to consult a lawyer (or maybe even your accountant) when deciding on a legal entity structure. It is also a good idea to use an experienced intellectual property lawyer if you are seeking to apply for a patent, trademark or copyright, or seeking to use something that may already be protected intellectual property.

So, yes, I think you should hire a lawyer.

What, if Any, Regulatory Compliance Issues Should I be Concerned With (especially for health and wellness start-ups)?

Because many of my law firm clients are health and wellness practition- ers, and because I see a lot of individuals wanting to start a coaching business, I thought it was important to dedicate a section of this book to those individuals. As I pointed out in my first book, *Rule the Rules of Workplace Wellness Programs*, health and wellness businesses are part of a highly regulated industry.

The cautionary tale that I like use is Theranos. Elizabeth Holmes was a very young entrepreneur when she founded Theranos, claiming the company could detect all kinds of health conditions with a single drop of blood. Likely because she was not a trained health clinician (she even dropped out of Stanford University after one year to pursue Theranos), Holmes did not appreciate all the regulatory hurdles that health and wellness companies must tackle if they want to be in business for the long term. The Theranos product failed to show scientific validity before being brought to market, and faced investigations and penalties from the Food and Drug Administration (FDA), the Centers for Medicare and Medicaid Services (CMS), the Securities Exchange Commission (SEC), and the Department of Justice (DOJ). Elizabeth Holmes not only lost her company and reputation, she is also facing criminal charges and a good possibility of spending significant time in prison.[19]

What does this mean for other aspiring health and wellness professionals? Well, it means that before starting your health or wellness venture, you must be aware of the legal landscape. Government oversight and penalties are very real in the health and wellness arena. And there are a lot of different government players of which to be aware. Here is a list of some of the government agencies that enforce compliance with health and wellness laws:

- Centers for Medicare and Medicaid Services (CMS)
- Food and Drug Administration (FDA)

---

[19] Lydia Ramsey Pflanzer, "The Rise and Fall of Theranos, the Blood Testing Start-Up that went from Silicon Valley Darling to Facing Fraud Charges," *Business Insider* (April 11, 2019), available at https://www.businessinsider.com/the-history-of-silicon-valley-unicorn-theranos-and-ceo-elizabeth-holmes-2018-5#soon-the-saga-will-be-portrayed-in-film-and-tv-adaptations-jennifer-lawrence-is-slated-to-play-holmes-in-a-film-directed-by-adam-mckay-while-kate-mckinnon-has-signed-on-to-play-holmes-in-a-hulu-series-39 (last visited July 12, 2020).

- Department of Justice (DOJ)
- Securities Exchange Commission (SEC)
- Federal Trade Commission (FTC)
- Office of Inspector General (federal and state)
- Office of Civil Rights (OCR)
- Equal Employment Opportunity Commission (EEOC)
- Department of Labor (DOL)
- Internal Revenue Service (IRS)
- State Departments of Health
- County/City Departments of Public Health
- State Insurance Commissioners
- State Consumer Protection Agencies
- State Professional Licensing Boards

This list does not include the private legal actions that consumers may take, such as malpractice or misrepresentation actions. There are

---

Whenever I tell people I'm a wellness lawyer, more often than not, they assume that I must know something about all different kinds of law, such as family law, criminal law, estate planning law, etc. The truth is, like many professions, lawyers specialize. The different bodies of law are vast and wide, and it is impossible for one person to be expert in all those areas. So, when you need a lawyer, don't assume he or she will be knowledgeable about all the different types of law you need to address for your business.

For example, if you meet a business lawyer, don't assume he or she can answer your questions about a speeding ticket or criminal indictment. Sure, all lawyers who went to law school had a class in criminal law, but it

(Continued on page 65)

---

numerous laws that each of the above agencies enforces. Some of the more common ones that I see as a practicing health and wellness attorney include:

- Health Insurance Portability and Accountability Act (HIPAA)
- Stark (Physician Self-Referral law)
- Anti-kickback
- Civil Monetary Penalties Law
- Food, Drug and Cosmetic Act (FDCA)
- Federal Trade Commission Act (FTCA)
- Medicare and Medicaid billing rules
- Americans with Disabilities Act (ADA)
- Title VII of the Civil Rights Act
- State privacy and security laws
- State scope of practice/unauthorized practice laws
- State telehealth laws

(Continued from page 64)
is a survey class that mostly teaches students how to "think like a lawyer." We don't memorize statutes. It is not until we start practicing that we begin to learn the specific language of certain laws and cases to help us guide clients. And this is usually confined to a specific practice area, which may be criminal law, general business law, litigation, real estate law, estate planning, family law, environmental law, tax law, mergers and acquisitions, intellectual property law, or in my case, health and wellness law. A competent lawyer will know their limits and refer you to the right person for areas in which he or she does not practice. This may be someone on their team, or they might need to refer outside their own firm.

- State corporate practice of medicine laws
- State professional licensing laws

Of course, this is not a comprehensive list, but it does show the wide array of federal and state laws that can be implicated in a health and wellness business.

If you are one of the many people who are interested in starting a health and wellness business, I highly recommend you partner with a competent health and wellness lawyer. General business lawyers do not likely know the intricacies and nuances of health and wellness laws. (See sidebar below.)

A case in point: One time, when I was negotiating a physician employee contract on behalf of a hospital system, the lawyer representing the physician was a general business lawyer. I was representing the hospital system as a health lawyer. The physician attended the negotiation with his lawyer. I noted that the contract did not address Stark law concerns (which are important concerns whenever working with physicians). The physician looked at his lawyer and asked, in front of me, if she knew anything about Stark and his lawyer said "no." He shook his head in disappointment and disbelief. Of course, I looked really smart, which was a real ego boost for a newly minted health lawyer. Moral of the story: If you are venturing into a health and wellness business, hire a health and wellness lawyer.

Also, for those of you who are thinking about starting a coaching practice, please find a competent lawyer to help your practice minimize its risk for potential malpractice or unlicensed practice allegations. Coaching is a wonderful profession, and it opens doors for so many people to share their knowledge and passion to a nationwide, and even international, audience. But, because coaching is not recognized by any state licensing board in the United States, you are at risk of complaints to licensing boards for unauthorized practice, particularly by those professionals who do hold such a license. They see you as a competitor and would like nothing more than to put you out of business. You can

CHAPTER FIVE

FUNDING

"SECURING FUNDING IS ONE OF THE hardest things you'll do as a business owner." That is a quote from Heather Wentler, Founder and Director for The Doyenne Group, a nonprofit organization that aims to help female entrepreneurs launch their businesses. And you know what? She is absolutely right. Remember all those wise words from people who have told you, "Get used to hearing the word 'no?'" Well, I think they are referring to potential funders of your idea.

In the first six months since starting Pursesuitz, I have been told "no" by potential funders each and every time. I have thus far applied for three different funding programs (two grants and one angel investor). My next stop may be a loan or self-financing on a smaller scale. But before I make a decision, I need more data. Let's talk about data, funding sources, and the reality of financing a new idea in this chapter.

I interviewed Heather Wentler to learn more about funding options for female entrepreneurs, but I also read a really good book called *Crack the Funding Code* by Judy Robinett. I highly recommend you check out Judy's book, but I will weave in some of the nuggets I learned in this chapter.

Before I jump into specifics, I want to share what my personal observation about the funding process. Other than what I wrote above about getting used to the word "no," the biggest observation I've had is that although it is never too early to start exploring funding options, you may not be ready for the "ask" until you have something tangible to show your potential funders.

It is important to remember that people "learn" in different ways. When asking for funding, you are "teaching" investors about your product or service. As with all types of learning, learning about a new product or service requires the ability to reach aural, kinesthetic, and visual learners. As a review, visual learners constitute about 65 percent of the population and learn best through images or the written word. Auditory learners constitute about 30 percent of the population and learn best through hearing. Finally, kinesthetic learners make up about five percent of the population and learn best through doing. See https://www.inc.com/molly-reynolds/how-to-spot-visual-auditory-and-kinesthetic-learni.html.

As a result, until you have a prototype to show your prospective funders, you won't be able to reach about 70 percent of the funder population because 65 percent will likely need to see your product and another five percent may need to actually use it or at least hold it in their hands.

I made that mistake with Pursesuitz. I applied for a grant way too early, before I even had a prototype made. I thought I did a stellar job describing in impressive detail how the shape-wear layer and outer layer would work, but no matter how good my description was, I was not reaching visual and kinesthetic learners. And I am a visual learner, so I should have known better! An actual prototype would also help kinesthetic learners because they would have something to touch and feel, and maybe even try on to see how the pockets work and their fantastic utility. The lesson here is that "yes," you should start thinking about funding as soon as possible, but you may not be able to successfully apply for those funds until you create a tangible product.

Moreover, as I learned in developing my prototype for Pursesuitz, you might need to go through several iterations before you land on a prototype that not only will appeal to potential funders, but even more importantly, will appeal to you. Sure, I thought I liked the first prototype with the two-layered blouse. But in all honesty, when I wore the two layers together, and felt the placement of the pockets, it was a bit uncomfortable, especially after wearing it for several hours and especially in warm weather.

Funding

It wasn't until I received more data from the focus groups and then improved upon the first protype with the second iteration of my product that I absolutely fell in love with the idea. The second version made so much more sense, and it was so much more comfortable. Once I reached that point, I felt proud of the result and much more confident in explaining it to potential funders.

If your business is selling a service, a visual aid to help investors or funders understand your approach to delivering the service may be a website, social media pages, or other promotional materials. A video describing your service, or better yet, showing how you deliver your service, may also help the visual learner. As for the kinesthetic learner, if you get the opportunity to role play a service scenario with the investor or funder, that may be a helpful approach.

But even with a visual aide, your funders may still say "no." They may want to see sales data or proof that that your concept will sell. This seems like an impossible situation. How can you start selling your concept to prove that people will buy it before you have money to get to the point where you are ready to sell? We'll explore that question and more in Chapter Eight. But, as far as searching for funding, don't give up, at least not until you get your proof (or lack thereof). This chapter discusses some ways to be creative with funding, as well as more conventional sources, such as:

- Grants
- Loans
- Angel investments
- Venture capital
- Crowd funding
- Personal funds or strategies.

Let's tackle each of them.

Grants

Believe it or not, there is grant money available for entrepreneurs. Grant money is the closest thing there is to "free money." You do not need to pay back grant money, but you do have to earn it in the form of an application and conditions on how you plan to spend it. For women entrepreneurs, there are a number of grant sources.

Here is a list of some small business grant opportunities, courtesy of Fundera.com:

- Grants.gov
- National Association for the Self-Employed Growth Grants (nase.org)
- Eileen Fisher Women-Owned Business Grant Program (eileenfisher.com/grants-overview)
- Amber Grant (ambergrantsforwomen.com)
- IdeaCafe Grant (businessownersideacafe.com)
- #GIRLBOSS Foundation Grant (girlboss.com)
- Cartier Women's Initiative Award (cartierwomensinitiative.com)
- GrantsforWomen.org
- FedEx Small Business Grant (fedex.com/en-us/smallbusiness/grant-contest.html)
- The Halstead Grant (for jewelry artists) (grant.halsteadbead.com)
- Open Meadows Foundation[20] (openmeadows.org)

This list is by no means exhaustive and the application process will differ for each grant. For example, the Amber Grant just wants to hear your story. You should make your story as compelling as possible, and try to tie in how your business not only solves a problem but makes the world a

---

[20] Rieva Lesonsky, *Small Business Grants for Women: 11 Incredible Opportunities* (Jan. 28, 2020), available at Fundera.com (last visited June 28, 2020).

better place (that has been my observation of winners thus far). Others require your business to be in operation for a certain number of years before applying, and yet others require a complete business plan before applying.

Loans

There are definite pros and cons to loans. The pros are that you maintain one hundred percent control of your business, giving you more freedom to decide how and when to move forward, and of course, less pressure to meet externally imposed targets or goals. The cons are that you take a hit to your credit score, you have to pay back what you borrow (plus interest), and you may put your personal assets at risk.

To apply for a loan, you must pull together a lot of documentation, including tax records, a personal financial statement, financial projections for your business (two to three years' worth), and a business plan, among other things. I have been told that this process can take about six weeks once you have submitted all of your documents. The lending institution's underwriters will examine all of your documentation and may ask you for more documentation if they still have questions. What they are evaluating is whether or not you are a good risk. Just like an investor, they want reassurance that their investment in you will pay off (i.e., they will at least get their money back, plus interest).

Some further bank-lending tips from Judy Robinett, author of *Crack the Funding Code*:

- Approach smaller community banks rather than big institutions. Small community banks (or credit unions) are more likely to learn about you and your business proposal, and thus, more willing to invest in you.

  I approached a local credit union that loans Small Business Administration (SBA) guaranteed loans. SBA-guaranteed loans are less risky for the lending institution, and sometimes include business counseling and better financing terms.

- Develop a relationship with your bank or credit union before you approach them for funding. For example, establish a checking and/or savings account with the bank or credit union, or a car loan or mortgage. The more the lender sees that you are a good risk, the more likely they will be willing to loan you money for your business.

- Only borrow the money that you need (don't overborrow). You will need to pay back the money you borrow, so try to keep loans to a minimum.[21]

Another source of loans may be women's business groups. I know that in Wisconsin, the Wisconsin Women's Business Initiative Corporation (WWBIC) loans SBA-guaranteed loans up to $250,000. Both men and women can apply. Other states may have similar organizations.

Also, banks usually want collateral, which means you must be willing to risk your business and/or your personal assets, depending on the bank and your situation. You will want to know up front what types of collateral the lending institution will want before signing any paperwork.

Angel and Venture Capital Investments

Unlike banks, angel investors and venture capital investors don't typically need collateral before investing in your business. I don't know about you, but I never really understood the difference between angel and venture capital investors until I read Judy Robinett's excellent book, *Crack the Funding Code*. According to Judy Robinett, angel investors are usually wealthy individuals who invest in new businesses in exchange for some equity in the business.[22] Angels can invest either as an individual or through a group, but most notably, they are a much more diverse crowd in terms of age, gender, and ethnicity.[23] Indeed, as noted by Heather Wentler of The Doyenne Group, also an angel investment group, angel

---

[21] Judy Robinett, *Crack the Funding Code: How Investors Think and What They Need to Hear to Fund Your Startup*, p. 37-38 (Harper Collins 2019).

[22] Ibid, p. 41.

[23] Ibid, p. 41.

investors are much more women-friendly than venture capital investment groups.[24] That is, angel investors are more likely to invest in women-owned businesses. Nevertheless, despite their reputation of being more women-friendly, less than 25 percent of angel investors are female.[25]

Another key difference between angel investors and venture capitalist investors is when they invest in a start-up. Angel investors are more likely to invest at an earlier stage of the start-up than a venture capital firm. Venture capital firms tend to invest much more money in a new company after the company has proven itself in the marketplace. In essence, venture capital can help take a growing and successful company to the next level.[256]

Venture capital firms typically invest other people's money, such as money from private foundations, pension plans, retirement funds, insurance companies, endowments, etc.[27] Venture capital firms typically invest millions of dollars in exchange for equity in your company, and they usually expect a 10-fold return on investment.[28] According to one expert, funding your business with venture capital is the most expensive cash.[28]

Granted, some companies reach a stage where venture capital is necessary and makes sense, but for many, obtaining money through venture capital creates pressure to perform at a certain level. For those of you who went into business to gain more control of your life, venture capital may erode some of that sense of freedom. The tradeoff of course is that the value of your company may increase, as well as your wealth. In addition, investors, whether angel or venture capital firms likely add some very savvy advisors to your team.

---

[24] Meeting with Heather Wentler, Executive Director of The Doyenne Group, in Madison, WI (March 26, 2020).

[25] Robinett, p 43-44.

[26] Ibid, p 44.

[27] Ibid. Robinett, p 44. See also Allen Brouwer and Cathryn Lavery, "Tim Ferriss Explains How to Scale Your Business in 3 Steps," *Entrepreneur* (Dec. 11, 2017).

[28] Ibid. Brouwer, Lavery.

How do you meet these investors? One good way is to join a business start-up group or class. You can Google entrepreneur classes or groups to find such opportunities in your community. It is very likely that part of the business group or class will include investors. Attending classes or meetings where investors are likely to hang out is a great way to introduce yourself, collect business cards and start building relationships with people who have money to invest.

In Wisconsin, my home state, the Wisconsin Technology Council runs the Wisconsin Investor Network (WIN). Individuals interested in connecting with investors can reach out to WIN, which can try to match you with an investor who might be a good fit for your business idea. There are usually similar groups to WIN in most other states.

Another good matchmaker for investors and startups owned by minorities or those who live in more rural communities is a Milwaukee-based venture called Uncrowd. Uncrowd is trying to make it easier for underrepresented groups in the start-up world to connect with investors. The company has created a platform with a database of business founders that investors can search to see if they are interested in investing in that startup. You can learn more about Uncrowd at https://uncrowd.io/.

You might also check with your local Chamber of Commerce or business associations to see if they have any leads. If you live near a university with a business school, faculty may have some ideas for you as well.

Crowdfunding

I love the idea of crowdfunding, especially for product-based businesses. Crowdfunding uses online platforms, such as Kickstarter, KIVA, and Indiegogo, to raise money from a lot of individuals who are interested in buying your product or service. For a small investment in your company, individuals who buy through crowdfunding get an early chance to get your product or service, many times for a discount, before it becomes widely available in the market. Individuals who frequent crowdfunding

74

platforms are looking for the next trendy product or service and want to get in on the ground floor.

Obviously, if you have an appealing product or service, you may raise a lot of money through crowdfunding. But even more importantly, you will have a pretty good idea if other people will be fans of your idea. So, I look at crowdfunding as a way to kill two birds with one stone: you have a chance to raise capital and you have confirmation of whether your idea will sell in the market.

Reviewing successful crowdfunding campaigns reveals that a catchy video helps attract potential buyers. Of course, well-produced videos are not cheap unless you, or friends and family, have video production skills. But video is a really good way to showcase your product or service in a short amount of time. So, be prepared to invest some time and money into making an impressive video.

Crowdfunding may be a good avenue for Pursesuitz. A video showing how the pockets can be used in multiple situations is essential for people to appreciate their versatility and usefulness. If I can produce such a video, I think I can garner interest from potential buyers for my product.

The beauty of crowdfunding is that you do not need to have an inventory to sell the product via a crowdfunding campaign. Instead, you can promise to deliver a product within a certain time period if an individual buys your product or service through the crowdfunding platform. So, if I crowdfunded Pursuitz Pocketwear Tanks, I could inform purchasers that their purchase is a preorder and that they will have their product, at a discount, within six weeks, for example. I would just need to leave enough time to gather some orders and give the manufacturer enough time to make the products. Of course, making a product through a pre-order method will not provide the manufacturing economies of scale that producing hundreds of pieces at once would provide.

But that is not really what crowdfunding is about. Crowdfunding is another way to test the market for your idea. If you have a successful crowdfunding campaign where you meet or exceed your funding goals, that is confirmation that your idea can succeed. You can use that evidence of success to obtain more funding through more traditional routes, such as bank loans, angel or venture capital investments or other funding sources.

Moreover, individuals who buy your product or service through crowdfunding can also provide feedback, allowing you to make improvements in future versions of your idea. They can also become part of your mailing list and social media page. It is important to make your social media accounts and crowdfunding pages work together. Make sure to link between the different platforms you use to get the word out about your idea. See Chapter Eleven for more about social media strategies.

Personal Funds or Strategies

The final way to get funding for your business is through "bootstrapping" or finding funds through friends, family, or yourself. I don't come from a wealthy family, so there was no way I could lean on anyone in my family to help invest in either my law firm or Pursesuitz. As for friends, I didn't feel comfortable asking any of them for financial help, and again, I don't have a lot of wealthy friends who are looking to invest money in other peoples' businesses. If you do have such friends or family, however, you may want to consider asking them for help.

Even if you are like me and do not have wealthy friends or family, some friends or family may be willing to invest time or talent. Indeed, as mentioned elsewhere in this book, you would be surprised how many people may be interested in becoming part of your idea by exchanging their talents or time for an equity stake in your business. If your idea resonates and you can sell it through your belief and passion, many people might want to join you for the ride.

Finally, there are always your own funds. You might have some savings or some items of value you can sell to help launch your business. If you own a home, you can borrow against your home's equity, or you can use credit cards. I don't necessarily advise maxing out your credit cards to finance a business, especially one that you aren't quite sure will work. I have witnessed friends get into serious debt through credit card overuse. If credit cards are your only option, my advice is to start small, and use the card only where it is absolutely necessary. If you can do something yourself, or find tools to help you learn so you can save money, consider going that route rather than hiring everyone to do all the different aspects of your business.

For example, when I started Pursesuitz, I cashed in some retirement savings to help me pay for social media help, website development, and of course, prototype development. In hindsight, I could have saved some money by doing some of these activities myself, or waiting a bit longer before investing in them.

Specifically, I should have waited for the website, for example, until the focus groups were complete. Having that feedback and then realizing I needed to pivot resulted in having to redo parts of the website, costing more money. I could have also used website developing tools to create a landing page, as I have done with other ventures of mine. One web development tool I have used in the past is webs.com. The website builder is quite intuitive and is a good way to get your idea out there without spending a lot of money. Once you have more traction in the marketplace, you can always revamp your website using a professional web-developing service.

With the Center for Health and Wellness Law, I used a personal loan to help me finance the start-up costs for a law firm. Luckily, there aren't many start-up costs for a law firm, as there is no inventory associated with legal services. The same is true for a coaching business or any number of other service-based businesses. The funds were helpful in acquiring some needed legal books and electronic resources, domain names, accounting services, a website, new computer, printer, and business cards. I also used a portion of the funds to finance some marketing activities, such as conference attendance and sponsoring some key events. Overall, however, the start-up expenses paled in comparison to what I need for Pursesuitz.

Regardless of how you seek money, according to Heather Wentler from The Doyenne Group, here are some things to do to prepare yourself to ask for money: [29]

- Have your own personal finances in order (even if that means if you have zero dollars).

- Figure out your personal budget as well as your business budget. Think of your business money as your capital, not just another bank account. You need to know how much money your company needs before you can quit your job.

- Set up forecasting and financial projections. Investors want to see financial projections up to five years out. That can be tricky to do in the very beginning, before you have any idea of how the market will respond to your idea. I made financial projections for Pursesuitz with the help of a consultant. I suggest doing the same if you don't have much familiarity with your market.

- Create an Executive Summary, which is a one- to two-page document giving a broad overview of your company, what growth looks like, and what your exit strategy may look like.

- Describe who is on your team. Your team members should bring experience and knowledge base to add or complement your own. Funders are not only vetting your company, but they are also vetting you. Do you have the right people on your team? Investors want to help and may make suggestions on who to add to your team. Your team can include advisors to show you have people you can go to. See Chapter Ten for a more in-depth discussion about finding the right team for you.

---

[29] Meeting with Heather Wentler, Executive Director of The Doyenne Group, in Madison, Wis. (March 26, 2020).

Funding

Funding is important, but it is not impossible. There are many options, some of which are described in this chapter, but likely many more exist. To know what is out there, however, you need to take that first step of moving your idea forward. Once you do, your eyes will open to the possibilities and opportunities that you would not see but for taking that step.

CHAPTER SIX
KNOW YOUR CUSTOMER

ONCE YOU HAVE SETTLED ON YOUR IDEA, it's time to survey the market. There are a lot of resources for conducting thorough market analyses, and many articles written about it as well. A good place to start to help you with your market research generally is the U.S. Small Business Administration. I found the website, https://www.sba.gov/business-guide/plan-your-business/market-research-competitive-analysis, extremely helpful. My suggested approach, however, is much more rudimentary. I don't recommend using my approach only. It is best to pair it with the multiple resources available on the Small Business Administration website.

To validate the strength of your idea, you should be familiar with your potential customer. One tool I stumbled across that appears very helpful in getting to know your customer is IBM's "Empathy Map." The Empathy Map is an activity you can do with a team of individuals (for example, your Advisory Board (see Chapter Ten)) to map out important traits of your potential customers. Empathy mapping is an activity that asks your team to answer the following questions about your potential customers:

- How do they feel?
- What do they say?
- What do they do?
- What do they think?

Each team member answers the questions independently. You then map out everyone's responses and look for themes and surprises. The team can then use these themes and surprises to better define your customer, and consequently, better define your messaging to them.

You can learn more about the Empathy Map activity at https://www.ibm.com/design/thinking/page/toolkit/activity/empathy-map.

Another way to get to know your customer is to answer the following questions about them:

- Who is she (or he, or they)?

- How many potential customers are out there?

- Would they buy my product or service? Why or why not?

- Assuming they would buy my product or service, why would they want to buy my product or service?

- How much would they be willing to pay for my product or service?

- Where are my potential customers? Specifically, where are they located geographically? Where are they online (to what social or professional groups do they belong?)?

- What message from me would grab their attention?

- Are there subgroups within my potential customer base? What message can I convey to grab the attention of each of those subgroups?

- Who is my competition?

- Why is my product or service better, in the eyes of my potential customer?

Those of us who are starting new ventures today as opposed to twenty years ago are lucky. We have the Internet and the multitude of resources that are now online. There is a wealth of information out there and it is really important to leverage that information as you continue on your ambitious journey.

I will use Pursesuitz and my law firm as test cases in answering the above ten questions. This may help show you how answering these questions for both a product-based business and a service-based business may lead you to conclusions you may not have had but for going through the questions yourself. This is a great exercise for anyone who is starting a new business.

Who is Your Potential Customer?

Pursesuitz

At first, I thought the ideal potential customer for Pursesuitz was all "ambitious" women. I thought that ambitious women would want to have clothing that let them be purse-free. I also thought that as these ambitious women learned why women's clothing did not have pockets, that they would be even more eager to buy clothing that let them be purse-free. I believed ambitious women would feel the same rage that I felt when I learned the discriminatory reasons why most women's clothing, to this day, does not have pockets: it is because women were not expected to have to carry anything important, and that they should not really be out and about without their husbands, who can carry the important items, anyway. There is a great video at cbsnews.com/video/the-500-year-history-of-the-pocket/#x that explains the history of pockets. I encourage every woman to watch it.

While ambitious women may still be my target market, as I researched the market, I realized that there is a segment of women who are already voicing their disappointment with carrying a purse or the lack of pockets in women's clothing. These women have organized social media groups, such as #womenwantpockets, or have commented on websites featuring articles by women who have ditched their purses. This subgroup of ambitious women—ambitious women who already are fed up with carrying a purse and longing for clothing with pockets—are my tribe. They are the ones already looking for my solution to their problem. So, when I am ready to launch my product, you can be sure I will be posting comments on the existing message boards, and joining the social media groups, and featuring my new product. As I mentioned earlier in the book, focusing on my tribe will be the most fulfilling way to launch my business because they will likely be most appreciative of the solution Pursesuitz provides.

The Center for Health and Wellness Law
My target customer has evolved over the past six years for my law firm. When I first started, I thought traditional healthcare providers and maybe some complementary and alternative care providers such as chiropractors would be my primary clients. But as I researched the market and attended conferences that attracted health and wellness providers, I realized that no lawyers were really focusing on wellness providers.

There is a wide range of wellness provider types, such as providers licensed in complementary and alternative medicine fields (such as chiropractic and acupuncture), as well as plenty of unlicensed providers (such as coaches, hypnotherapists, and more "spiritual" healers). These providers are usually solo practitioners and start-ups, and so would not be on the radar of traditional law firm health law departments. Yet, these providers need legal guidance. I decided that those providers would be my target clients and started directing my messaging in blogs, social media, and presentations toward them.

How Many Potential Customers are Out There?

Pursesuitz
If I were lazy, I could say half the population, because half the population is women. But I am not really aiming to sell to all women. As noted in the response to the previous question, my tribe is women who already find purses an annoyance and want or need clothing with functional pockets. That is a much narrower group. So how do I count them?

One way to gauge the market is to look at purse sales. According to one source, purse sales have dropped in recent years in favor of backpacks and fanny packs. In fact, backpack sales for women increased by 15 percent and fanny packs by 52 percent in 2018.[30] This is particularly true in large city environments, where many women use public transport to commute to work. Having their hands free to hold a coffee, phone or nothing, is a valuable perk. Plus, not carrying a purse over one shoulder avoids putting unnecessary stress on the back.

So, translating this information for Pursesuitz, I know that women who are buying backpacks may also be interested in buying a top that can keep their most essential items, like their phone, wallet, and keys, accessible on their person at all times, while allowing them to use their backpack for items such as workout clothes, laptops, iPads, headphones, sneakers, or other items that don't necessarily have to be at the ready. Pursesuitz can capitalize on this trend in backpack purchases by cross-marketing with backpack manufacturers.

To get an idea of the market size for handbags and tops, I explored Statista.com, which offers market insight into a variety of products and services. For a fee, you can get even more information, but I just used the free data for now.

From Statista, I learned that the "bags and accessories" market in the United States is projected to have revenue of $142 million in 2020, and that revenue is expected to show an annual growth rate of 10.8 percent, resulting in a market volume of $214 million by 2024. I also learned that online sales of bags and accessories is only 26 percent of the market, but growing every year.

That said, the "hero" product for Pursesuitz is a top with pockets, so it is important to also examine the market of women's clothing. Statista has statistics on those markets as well. The women's suits and ensembles market is a bit smaller than the bags and accessories market. Revenue for

---

[30] Richard Kastenbaum, "Handbag Sales are Down—Here's What Consumers are Buying Instead," Forbes, Oct. 17, 2018. See also NPD, "Outerwear, Fanny Packs and Other Bags Drive US Outdoor Industry Sales," Nov. 5, 2018.

2020 for suits and ensembles is projected to be $9.1 million. The market for women's shirts and blouses is projected to be $82 million in revenue for 2020, with an annual growth rate of 4.3 percent between 2020 and 2023. Because the "hero" product for Pursesuitz also functions like a bra, it is important to also look at the market for underwear. According to Statista, the market for women's night and underwear is $89 million in 2020, with an annual growth rate of 4.4 percent between 2020 and 2023.

The hero product is made out of shapewear, so it could also be marketed in the athleisure market. According to Report linker, another source for market research, the athleisure market is expected to grow by 6.7 percent from 2019 to 2026.[31]

Moreover, "fashionable athleisure products have witnessed a surge in demand"[32] from female consumers. I am sure that COVID-19 increased the interest in athleisure even more, since remote work has become the new norm and business attire is likely not as in demand as pre-COVID-19 days.

Based on this data, the market category that has the most growth potential is the bags and accessories category. Second in line is the athleisure market. It might make sense, then, to look at potential customers of women's backpack, fitness, and travel markets. Although Pursesuitz tops are not backpacks, they could be cross-marketed with backpacks to show how pairing a backpack with a Pursesuitz top enhances the "hands-free" experience. This would allow women to use their backpacks for larger items and the Pursesuitz top for their essential items that should be kept close for convenience and safety. Pairing with a backpack also makes sense for women who are traveling or working out through hiking, biking, or walking.

---

[31] *PRNews Wire*, Reportlinker, The athleisure market size was valued at $155.2 billion in 2018 and is expected to reach $257.1 billion by 2026, registering a CAGR of 6.7% from 2019 to 2026 (Dec. 2, 2019), available at https://www.prnewswire.com/news-releases/the-athleisure-market-size-was-valued-at-155-2-billion-in-2018-and-is-expected-to-reach-257-1-billion-by-2026--registering-a-cagr-of-6-7-from-2019-to-2026--300967335.html (last visited October 3, 2020).

[32] Ibid.

Thus, by exploring the numbers of potential customers, Pursesuitz is able to not only assess the size of the market, but also explore potential marketing avenues that may not have been thought of before, such as cross-marketing with ladies' backpack, athletic, or travel products.

Of course, as I mentioned earlier in this book, I also don't want to limit the use of my product by putting it in a certain category like travel or athleisure. As a result, I also plan to market my product through a newly created category: Pocketwear. I am a big believer in creating platforms when the current menu of options falls short. Who knows? Pursesuitz Pocketwear may become the next Kleenex of brands!

The Center for Health and Wellness Law

Using my health and wellness coaches as my primary target client, the statistics show that this is a booming field. With good reason. My own personal experience with traditional healthcare demonstrates a need for individuals who can help educate about health and wellness, and support health and wellness goals. I tried to get such education and support from my primary-care doctor, but to no avail. Particularly in COVID-19, traditional healthcare is overextended, and prevention and education are not high on the priority list.

Health and wellness coaches can fill that void by being available for education and support. With the growth of telemedicine, health and wellness coaches can help individuals all over the world. Health and wellness coaches do not need a state-issued license to offer services, and can avoid regulatory trouble as long as they "stay in the coaching lane" and avoid drifting into a licensed practice area (most often medicine, psychotherapy, or dietetics).

According to the Market Research Blog by John LaRosa,[33] health coaching has emerged as a $6 billion service market, with a strong growth

---

[33] John LaRosa, Health Coaching Gains Favor Among Consumers, Insurers, and Employers, Market Research Blog (June 6, 2018), available at https://blog.marketresearch.com/health-coaching-gains-favor-among-u.s.-consumers-insurers-employers (last visited October 3, 2020).

trajectory. Health coaching is expected to grow at a 5.4 percent average annual pace, growing from 109,000 health coaches and educators in the U.S. from 2018 to 121,000 coaches in 2022.[34] Many health coaches are in private practice, so of course, they need a legal partner to help their business grow and stay compliant. The Center for Health and Wellness Law is in a prime position to be that legal partner in the market.

For your product or service, what are some similar or complementary markets that you can explore to help determine the size of your market, and perhaps help you think of new ways to sell, or cross-sell, your product or service?

Would Potential Customers Buy My Product or Service? Why or Why Not?

Pursesuitz

This seems like a silly question. "Of course my potential customers will buy my product or service! Why else would I be pursuing this idea?" Well, the purpose of this question is to force us to look beyond our own beliefs. It's a hard thing to do, especially when you are just getting started, and when you are trying to keep the faith. However, don't look at the survey as confirmation of your idea, but rather idea improvement. The feedback you get from surveys may refine your idea to something even better than your original vision, which is what happened with Pursesuitz.

So, what are some ways you can survey your potential customers? Here are some ideas:

- Join a relevant social media group and post a question to the group.

- Join an entrepreneurship and/or networking group on social media and pose your question there. (Entrepreneurs are eager to help other entrepreneurs).

---

[34] LaRosa, blog.

- Join a trade association and find out if you can survey the group. You might have to pay for an email list, but it might be worth it to have a built-in customer list like that.

- Host an event and invite potential customers to give you their feedback in person. The event might be something unrelated to your business, but can help entice people to attend. I did this when I started at my previous law firm. I held a chocolate-tasting event with a local chocolatier. I invited all kinds of people to my new law firm for the event. A lot of people attended, and I was able to showcase my new law practice at my new firm. The same idea could work for any start-up.

- Ask potential customers as you meet them while out and about. Whenever I meet someone new, as long as it feels appropriate, I try to gauge their interest in the Pursesuitz Pocketwear Tank. Usually, the response has been very positive, which is reassuring. And whenever I am wearing my prototype, I try to show them its usefulness.

What should you ask your potential customers in your survey? Ask them at least the following questions:

- Describe your product or service, and ask if they would be interested in it.

- For those who answer, ask them how much would they be willing to pay for the product or service (ask them via multiple choice rather than leave it open-ended and use numbers you could live with).

- For those who answer in the negative (they would not be interested in your product or service), ask them why.

- For those who answer in the negative, ask them if there is anything that would change their mind.

For Pursesuitz, I conducted focus groups to get their feedback, rather than conducting a survey. Because of the product needing to appeal to a variety of senses, such as sight, touch and fit, having the potential customers try on the product was essential. Focus groups were a good way to allow that to happen.

Center for Health and Wellness Law

I have had clients buy my legal and compliance services, but when I first started my firm, I wasn't sure who all would buy my services and for how much. I conducted an informal survey by attending events where many of my target clients would be. While there, I asked attendees what they knew about the law as it pertained to health and wellness services. To my surprise, many responses indicated that they knew very little but craved a comprehensive resource for "wellness law." I also observed that there were no lawyers attending these events. So, I started calling associations for wellness professionals who hosted these events and asked if they needed a legal expert to speak or write to their members. Again, to my pleasant surprise, they said "yes," and that they had been waiting for someone like me to step forward and fill that slot.

Because members of my target client base informed me that they needed legal resources, I assumed that they would be willing to pay for those resources. I set the price for my services based on what I knew other law firms were charging, but at a slightly lower rate. That way, my clients would feel like they were getting good value, even though there really wasn't any real competition in the wellness law marketplace. Seven years into my law practice, I am still filling a void by specializing in wellness law.

Assuming They Would Buy My Product or Service, Why Would They Buy My Product or Service?

Pursesuitz

This question really gets you thinking about your story or your mission. When I first told people about Pursesuitz, they seemed interested, but not really excited. Based on the feedback from the focus groups, I think the lukewarm reception was the result of mistaken assumptions about my target market. I thought that the original purpose behind Pursesuitz—to achieve equality in the workplace through stylish business attire with pockets—would resonate with my target market. It didn't. It was too much of a leap to go from blouses with pockets to equality in the workplace. The messaging needed to get the customers to that place of understanding was too challenging and couldn't be done with a pithy, punchy tag line. They also weren't crazy about the two layers, the placement of the pockets, or the price point. So I had to re-evaluate my mission.

The focus groups informed me that they would be interested in my product for travel or leisure purposes, because the inner layer pockets seemed like a good alternative to carrying a bag or purse. So, I changed my mission to focus on the pockets. Pockets are what makes the Pursesuitz hero product stand out. It is a top that can function as underwear or athleisure wear with functional pockets. Pockets give you security, convenience, and freedom. Freedom for your hands, freedom from shoulder pain caused by carrying a bag, freedom from worry about losing your essential items, and freedom to wear whatever you want with the product and still have pockets. That's the messaging I have decided will resonate most. And I believe it will resonate most with women who already yearn for clothing with pockets, such as those who run, bike, hike, or travel. Therefore, the mission has changed to make Pursesuitz Pocketwear—versatile clothes with functional pockets for women.

The Center for Health and Wellness Law

Clients buy legal and compliance services from my law firm first and foremost because there really aren't any other legal professionals who specialize in wellness law, which is a terrific position in any market. I created the term "wellness law" and own the domain name, so I have freedom to create the market of services that I see fit.

Of course, clients could always seek the assistance of lawyers who identify with more traditional practice areas, such as employee and benefits law, or health law. And some potential clients do go that route. By marketing specifically to health and wellness professionals, particularly the solo practitioners and start-ups, many potential clients see my firm first as a legal partner. Because I specialize in health and wellness law, clients feel like I understand their work and their goals, and that makes them feel more comfortable using my firm over firms that cater to clients from a wide variety of industries.

What is it about *your* product or service that makes it stand out compared to other options? Think about your purpose behind offering your product or service to find that unique feature that will make your idea stand out from the crowd. Is it your own personal story that differentiates your idea? Or, is it something about the way you deliver your service or make your product that separates it from the rest? Once you find your uniqueness, capitalize on it. Make it part of your brand. Tell your story on social media, on your website, on YouTube, or maybe even write a book! See Chapter Eight for more on finding your uniqueness.

How Much Would My Customers be Willing to Pay for My Product or Service?

Pursesuitz

As part of your survey, whether it's an impromptu in-person survey with someone, a focus group, or a written survey, it's a good idea to ask potential customers how much they would be willing to spend on your product or service. If possible, give them multiple choice answers with a range of possible price points.

The information you gather from potential customers will be useful, but it should not be the sole basis for your decision on price. After all, when you are first starting out, it may be really hard to accurately value your product or service. You will know, however, how much it costs to make.

Sara Blakely advises in her Masterclass that your price should be five times what it costs to make. That is much easier said than done, especially when you are first starting out. Don't get me wrong, it would be nice to be able to sell your product at five times the production cost, but it may not be realistic. I am learning this as I launch Pursesuitz.

Producing my prototype is costing a lot more than mass producing my hero product. In the prototype stage, I am using a manufacturer based in the United States, and I am only making a few samples. This means the cost of production is quite high. Let's say it costs $50 to produce one hero product using the current U.S-based manufacturer. If I were to sell my hero product at five times the cost, that would price my product at $250. I'm sorry, very few women would spend $250 for a tank top, even if it is made from fabulous material and has pockets!

Based on market research that I have done with similar products, such as Spanx, I know that consumers may buy a shapewear tank for around $65. That isn't even double of what it costs to produce. However, I am willing to take the financial hit early on until I see enough orders to produce for a much lower cost. Once you start producing hundreds or thousands of product, the cost of production decreases significantly, which increases your profit margin. One may assume that the "five times production cost" price suggestion means when you are able to produce hundreds or thousands of product at a time.

Center for Health and Wellness Law

As for how to price a service-based business, market research should include learning what similar businesses charge for their services. When I priced my services for the Center for Health and Wellness Law, I knew how much other law firms charged because I had worked in other law firms and knew what they charged for my hourly rate. You may not have that luxury, but asking potential customers and fellow providers of similar services can probably arm you with the price information you need.

That being said, I have seen entrepreneurs of service-based businesses set their price to only attract a certain clientele, i.e., wealthy ones. That may sound like a great strategy, but if you aim only for wealthy clients, I believe you miss out on some really great opportunities. A case in point is law firms that require upfront payments of hundreds of dollars before the client can even consult with a lawyer. Many potential

> **Practical Tip**
> For service-based businesses, make sure you include language in your service agreement that permits you to increase the price for your services on at least an annual basis. You don't have to, but it gives you the option to stay on top of changes in the economy.

clients cannot afford hundreds of dollars just for the opportunity to speak with a lawyer to see if the lawyer or law firm is a good fit. I believe offering free 15-minute consultations to determine if the client relationship is a good match for your business is a better approach because it allows you as the business owner and the potential client a chance to preview the relationship without investing a lot of time and money. Most of the time, requiring clients to pay upfront before even speaking to you just causes immediate tension and impossible expectations.

I think it is best for service-based businesses just starting out to price your services in the middle of the market. It is easier to justify your value when your price is in the middle of what others charge for similar services.

Where Are My Potential Customers?
(Specifically, where are they located geographically?
Where are they online?
To what social or professional group(s) do they belong?)

It is vital to know where to find your customers, both in person and online. Are your potential customers in cities, in rural areas, near the coast, or in the heartland? Or, does it not matter where your customers are located? Perhaps your product or service caters to people regardless of location. Knowing where your customers are located helps with your market research, such as finding your competitors and the prices they charge for similar products or services.

For businesses that have a geographic market, you will need to research where your potential customers live and work. If you have a brick-and-mortar business model, a convenient location for your customers may be critical if those customers must travel to your building to access your products or services. The more unique your business, the farther your potential customers will be willing to travel to get to you. A good resource I have found for researching basic measures, such as income, housing profiles, resident age, gender, race, and profiles of local businesses by zip code is www.city-data/com. The website is free!

If you have no geographic restrictions on customers, then finding their online locations is gold. Are there social media or professional groups to which your potential customers belong? Or are there already-existing websites or chat groups where your potential customers congregate? Knowing where to find your target market is half the battle to successful marketing.

Pursesuitz

As I look for my potential customers for Pursesuitz, I am finding a number of social media groups, as well as chat groups, through Google where women are complaining about either: 1) carrying a purse; or 2) not having functional pockets in their clothing. I believe both types of women would be very interested in learning about Pursesuitz clothing. Also, groups interested in travel, sports, and fitness would be interested in my product, and such groups are plentiful on social media. Hence, it will be important to get in front of those groups to find ways to communicate with their members. One good way to get started is to write or record a message that will resonate with those groups. Offering to write for a group's magazine or blog site is a good way to get in front of group members as those groups are usually always hungry for content.

Center for Health and Wellness Law

Potential clients for my law firm belong to certain wellness associations, as well as social media groups. Presenting, posting, and writing for these groups, as well as just writing relevant blog posts for my website, are a great way to attract the attention of these potential clients. Because my law firm handles a lot of federal law, my clients can be anywhere in the United States.

Who are your potential customers, and where can you find them in person or online? Write down your answers and then start reaching out to them!

What Message from My Company Will Grab My Potential Customers' Attention?

This gets back to finding your niche or unique slant to your business idea. Once you land on your unique style or position, you should think of a succinct, catchy way to tell people about your idea and why they should buy from you and no one else.

To find an effective message, consider current trends, as well as popular messaging channels. But also consider more fundamental messages that perhaps tug at people's heart strings, or ignite an inner, universal desire within your customer population. Social media offers a treasure trove of information to gauge what gets people excited. Are there trending #hashtags you can use to capture the attention of your potential audience? Are there issues your potential customers talk about, or inherently care about? List what those issues or trends might be and then try to craft a message about your product or service that incorporates that message.

When I worked at my former law firm, one marketing skill they asked us to master was our "elevator pitch." We were challenged to come up with a very succinct, powerful message to answer the question: "What do you do?" They called it an elevator pitch because you should be able to recite the pitch in the time it takes you to ride up or down a typical elevator, which may only be a few floors. So, no more than 30 seconds long. But I think shorter is even better. Just like writing, it is more difficult to convey a message in few words than more words.

Communicating in as few words as possible requires you to find the perfect words to capture the best meaning for your message. Here are the slogans I use for my businesses.

Center for Health and Wellness Law

The slogan for my law firm is "Improving Legal Access and Compliance for Health and Wellness Providers." I chose to include the word "access" because I wanted to emphasize that my firm is more affordable and focused on health and wellness providers. I chose "compliance" because I wanted to emphasize that my firm specializes in health and wellness compliance, as opposed to litigation or other more adversarial work. Finally, I made sure to include my target client, "health and wellness providers," so that it is more clear that I help providers, and not patients of providers.

Pursesuitz

The initial slogan I chose for the Pursesuitz was "Pursuing Gender Equality, with Style." The slogan aimed to appeal to my customers' desire to be equal to men, as well as their desire to look professional. However, that message did not resonate with the focus groups because they could not readily make the connection between the absence of pockets and gender inequality. My intent behind the slogan was to point out that men's clothing almost always has functional pockets, while women's clothing does not. This stems from decisions made hundreds of years ago that women didn't need pockets because they shouldn't be outside the home, and if they did venture out, they would be with their husband who could carry essential items in his pockets.

My focus group attendees had difficulty making that connection, and it would take more than a snappy slogan to help them get there. That was an important lesson for me to learn: customers have not done the same amount of research as me, so there may be a significant gap in the messaging that is not easy to fill with a snappy slogan.

If that is the case with your business idea, try to think of a slogan that expresses the prominent feature of your unique idea. For Pursesuitz, that unique idea was functional pockets in a tank top, giving the wearer more freedom and security when moving about. That is why I have now selected Pursesuitz Pocketwear as my message. I'm not sure it really qualifies as a slogan, but the simple message conveys what I think will appeal most to potential buyers. I have decided to make the gender equality message secondary to the Pocketwear message. I am hopeful that women who buy Pursesuitz will still feel like they are making a statement in support of gender equality.

> **Practical Tip**
> Wait to purchase business cards or other items showcasing your slogan until you've tested it in the market. I made the mistake of purchasing labels and tags before conducting the focus groups. The feedback from the focus groups led me to change my slogan, which meant I had to purchase new labels and tags with the new motto.

Think about how you can create a short, memorable message about your product or service. Enlist your friends and family to help you find a message, once you've done the hard work of identifying your uniqueness in the market. You will be amazed at how brainstorming can lead to some very valuable information and results.

Are There Subgroups Within My Potential Customer Base? (What message can I convey to grab the attention of each of those subgroups?)

If thinking of a message to your total customer base seems daunting, it might be easier to think of a message to a smaller segment of your customer population.

Pursesuitz

For Pursesuitz, the total customer population, theoretically speaking, is women. But within that large group are smaller subgroups, such as women who hate purses, or women who want functional pockets, or women who want to carry a backpack to work so that their hands are free, or women who are on the go while at home and work and need to have their phone on their person at all times so they don't miss important calls, or in the era of Coronavirus, women who want to avoid contaminating their purse or phone while in public places. I could create separate messages for each of these groups, as shown in the following table:

Table 5.1

Pursesuitz Subgroup	Potential Attention-Grabbing Message
Women who hate purses	Pursesuitz: Pocketwear clothing for a purse-free life
Women who want functional pockets	Pursesuitz: Pocketwear clothing that holds your most essential items
Women who carry backpacks	Pursesuitz: Pocketwear clothing for your hands-free life
Women on the go	Pursesuitz: Pocketwear clothing so you never miss another text or call
Women who want to feel safe and avoid germs	Pursesuitz: Pocketwear clothing to keep your items safe and germ-free.

Center for Health and Wellness Law ("Center")

Creating the tables above for both Pursesuitz and the Center for Health and Wellness Law was a really good exercise. *You should try it!* Thinking of "sub-messages" solidified the utility of my businesses from different perspectives. Knowing that my businesses can help clients solve all kinds of different problems energizes me to keep moving forward with my businesses. In these early stages of starting a business, it is so important to stay motivated. Each exercise, like finding messages for subgroups, takes you one step closer to fulfilling your dream.

Table 5.2

Center Subgroup	Potential Attention-Grabbing Message
Health and wellness coaches	The Center specializes in helping health and wellness coaches thrive – legally!
Licensed health professionals	The Center is your best resource for navigating the health law landscape.
Wellness professionals and companies	A law firm that knows and appreciates what you do.

Who is My Competition?

Knowing your customer also requires knowing your competition. In fact, knowing who else your customer might buy from provides insight into what your potential customers want. Your competition may not necessarily be a business selling the exact same type of product or service as you. Competition can take many different forms. And sometimes, who you think might be your competition could actually be an ally.

Center for Health and Wellness Law

For example, with my first business, the Center for Health and Wellness Law, LLC, my competition did not turn out to be other law firms. Because I was operating in a very niche practice area—wellness law—very few other law firms had such a practice area. Instead, I learned over time that my real competition was insurance brokers. Insurance brokers were the ones to whom employers often turned to find workplace wellness programs for their employees. Employers then also turned to those same brokers for legal or compliance advice about those wellness programs.

Wellness compliance advice was exactly the service I was offering in the workplace wellness market! Because I knew many insurance brokers did not have wellness law expertise, however, I marketed to them. In a way, then, my legal services helped train the "trainers," who were the insurance brokers. I also wrote a book and created a compliance course to market to the wellness industry, including many insurance brokers.

Pursesuitz

For Pursesuitz, my competition is not just other women's clothing companies. Because of the multi-purpose nature of my hero product, my competition is likely also to be underwear companies, athleisure wear companies, as well as handbag and fanny pack companies. This is because my product serves multiple purposes: it functions as a purse, a bra, and exercise clothing. Thus, I must consider reaching out to customers who shop for all three of those types of products. I must also research the price points for those three different products and tailor my marketing messages to fit within those three different products. In a way, examining my competition also identifies potential customer subgroups. I have added these three new subgroups to Table 5.1:

This topic of knowing your competitors is explored further in the next chapter.

Amended Table 5.1

Pursesuitz Subgroup	Potential Attention-Grabbing Message
Women who hate purses	Pursesuitz Pocketwear: clothing for a purse-free life
Women who want functional pockets	Pursesuitz Pocketwear: clothing that holds your most essential items
Women who carry backpacks	Pursesuitz Pocketwear: clothing for your hands-free life
Women on the go	Pursesuitz Pocketwear: clothing so you never miss another text or call
Women who want to avoid germs	Pursesuitz Pocketwear: clothing to keep your essential items safe and germ-free.
Women who want purses	Wear your purse for "just in case," and Pursesuitz for style and ease.
Women who need underwear	Pursesuitz: Underwear for form and function
Women who want athletic wear	Athletic wear with function and a mission Pursesuitz Pocketwear: better than a fitness belt
Women who wear fanny packs	Don't sacrifice style for convenience: Get both with Pursesuitz Pocketwear!

Why is My Product or Service Better
in the Eyes of my Potential Customer?

Knowing your customer means knowing what they care about and how you can channel that care into your messaging. Identifying customer subgroups can help you consider your customer's concerns or desires and then tailor your messaging to address those concerns and desires. By effectively addressing customer concerns and desires, you are on your way to differentiating your product or service from your competition.

Differentiating your product or service also gets back to finding your unique purpose, background, or approach to your product or service. Celebrating that uniqueness and making that part of your messaging aims to convince your customers about why they should pick your product or service over others. As a result, try to weave your uniqueness into all of your marketing; don't let it get lost. This is discussed further in Chapter Eight.

To help you find a satisfying message for your venture, try the following exercise.

EXERCISE: ANSWER THE FOLLOWING QUESTIONS

1. Who are your customers, including subgroups of customers?

2. What are their desires or concerns?

3. How do they currently solve those desires or concerns?

4. How can your product or service address those desires or concerns?

5. Given your answers to the above questions, what succinct message could you convey about how your product or service addresses those desires or concerns?

Congratulations!

You just took the first step in creating an effective message for your new venture!

CHAPTER SEVEN

KNOW YOUR COMPETITION

Know Internal Competition

KNOWING YOUR COMPETITION HELPS YOU know your own business and your unique place in the world. But who is your competition? It may not be as obvious as you might think. In fact, I would argue that your biggest competition is YOU. Yes, that's right. If we define a competitor as someone or something that gets in the way of your success, that steals attention away from your business, then it is easy to see how you can be your biggest competitor. So, knowing yourself is absolutely critical to your business's success.

Let me put this into more context. When I started Pursesuitz, I had big visions for what it could be, and that is good. Aiming high is what most successful people will tell you. But as you move through the process of building your business, dreams intersect with reality and sometimes reality doesn't always align with your dreams. Life happens and let's face it, you are human, which means you are vulnerable to what life throws at you. Maybe someone in your family gets sick, maybe you lose your day job, or maybe another great idea comes along calling into question whether your "big ambition" is really the right "big ambition."

After I created the first prototypes of Pursesuitz clothing, I tested the clothes through conducting a few focus groups. Each focus group included my target consumer: women between age 35 and 55 who were climbing to the top of their careers. Their feedback was extremely valuable, but also shocking. Overall they loved the concept, but they weren't likely to buy it and they certainly were not interested in giving up their purses (except for one attendee who like me, hates purses). This was tough to hear. As one of my law firm mentors may have told me if he were still alive, I was "drinking my own Kool-Aid." I believed in my product so much that I couldn't fathom anyone else not liking it as much as me. But that was not the case.

This feedback threw my whole idea into peril. I began to question whether Pursesuitz was the right idea I should be pursuing. While I had been pouring so much money and energy into Pursesuitz, my other business, the Center for Health and Wellness Law, was humming along, even growing! I thought perhaps I should be pouring more of myself into my law firm. Then, I started recalling all the other ideas I had over the years that suddenly seemed to have more appeal and potential.

One of those other ideas includes Lemonspark. Through the entrepreneurship process of Pursesuitz, I began to learn more about me. Like many serial entrepreneurs, I have a lot of what I think are "great ideas," but not enough bandwidth to tackle them all (at least not all at once). Lemonspark was something I started a long time ago and then put it on the backburner as my life became very busy and other priorities took over. I've always thought it was a good idea, however, and I began to wonder if it wasn't time to revive it given the cool reception of Pursesuitz.

But, then again, I had invested so much time and money in exploring Pursesuitz, that if I just pivoted based on the feedback, maybe I could still make it work. I thought about focusing only on the inner layer, rather than two layers, giving the inner layer more versatility, which is what some women in the focus group wanted. Specifically, they thought the concept was better suited for travel and leisure purposes, not work. Focusing on improving the inner layer so that it could be worn for travel, leisure, or work may make the product more appealing to a wider audience, and it is less expensive to make one layer instead of two.

And this is what I mean by YOU are your biggest competition. The thoughts racing through my head about quitting, pivoting, or focusing on other projects were taking me away from Pursesuitz's success. Sure, there were other "external" competitors for Pursesuitz, like other shapewear companies and countless fashion companies. But, my ability or inability to believe in my idea through thick and thin was the most impactful competition.

I could navigate external competition through specialized branding (see Chapter Nine). But beating internal competition depends solely on my ability to convince myself that my venture is worth pursuing, and that requires some excruciating soul searching. To start the soul searching, consider going through the external competition analysis for your own idea, as outlined below.

Know Your External Competition

For those of you who have done that soul-searching and landed with continuing your big ambition, there are some great resources to research your potential competition. For example, the Small Business Administration (SBA) website has a competitive research tool available at: https://www.sba.gov/business-guide/plan-your-business/market-research-competitive-analysis.

There, you can find another link to Porter's Five Forces. The five-forces perspective is associated with its originator, Michael E. Porter of Harvard University. Porter's Five Forces look at the economy of industry you are trying to break into and provides "a framework for anticipating and influencing competition (and profitability) over time."[34] Porter's Five Forces are:

1. Competitive Rivalry

2. The Bargaining Power of Suppliers

3. The Bargaining Power or Customers

4. The Threat of New Entrants

5. The Threat of Substitute Products or Services

---

[34] Marci Martin, How Porter's Five Forces can Help Small Businesses Analyze the Competition, *Business Insider* (Dec. 3, 2019), available at https://www.businessnewsdaily.com/5446-porters-five-forces.html.

Porter's Five Forces can lead you down a path of really evaluating your commitment and the viability of your idea. It is a good place to start the soul-searching process if you still aren't sure whether your idea will fly (and whether you really want it to fly). Let's explore each force in turn.

1. Competitive Rivalry

Are there already a lot of businesses in this space? How easily can your customers switch to a competitor if they don't like your product or service? Are there a lot of new entrants into this market? If your answers are "yes" to these questions, then plan on spending a lot of money on advertising and taking cuts to your profit margin in order to become competitive.

Let's apply this force to my businesses.

Pursesuitz

The primary product is the inner shapewear layer. There are a lot of shapewear companies in the marketplace, and looking at social media advertisements, they seem to be growing in number. Of course, none of them are placing pockets at the waist of a tank top made of compression fabric, but there are alternatives to those pockets through different-sized purses. The question will be whether the customer wants to be free of her purse. I am banking on that. Indeed, after more market research, I've decided to focus on women who need no convincing that purses are inconvenient. Women who are active and who travel already share that mindset, so targeting them and the products they may turn to, such as running belts or fanny packs, will direct my marketing strategy. There is also the possibility that the shapewear rivals will start making pockets in their products. Branding and protecting my design will be key to stand out in that crowd.

Center for Health and Wellness Law

Because I am so specialized in the legal and compliance services I provide, there are no real competitors for the specific area of law I practice: wellness law. However, my law firm also provides other legal and compliance services, such as general business law for health and wellness clients. There are plenty of other lawyers who provide general business legal services. If I viewed my law firm as a general business law firm, the market would be saturated and it would be very difficult and expensive to make my firm stand out in the crowd. But if health and wellness clients are looking for a firm that caters to their specific market, any Google search for "wellness law" or "wellness attorney" is likely to bring up my law firm in the search. So, how you see yourself and your competition impacts your competitive rivalry analysis.

2. The Bargaining Power of Suppliers

This force looks at how many suppliers there are to make your product. Are there a lot of suppliers of materials from which you can choose, or only a few? If just a few, then those suppliers have more bargaining power and can raise their prices more easily, cutting into your profits. If, however, there are a lot of choices of suppliers, then your business may be in a better place because you can switch suppliers if their prices get too high.

Pursesuitz

My suppliers include fabric suppliers, clothing label suppliers, pattern makers, and sewers (manufacturers). I also need to rely on freelance clothing designers to help me create the samples. Overall, there seems to be a lot of suppliers for these types of inputs to my product, but the more I specialize, such as with recycled compression fabric, the list of potential suppliers shrinks.

Center for Health and Wellness Law

Because it is a service business, there is not much overhead in the way of supplies. One of the biggest expenses is legal research, but even much of that can be done with free or very inexpensive search tools. Thus, there are quite a few options for legal research tools, so profit margins are not likely to taking that big of a hit.

3. The Bargaining Power of Customers

This force really has to do with the uniqueness of your product or brand. If consumers have a lot of choices in buying what you sell, the consumer has more bargaining power when it comes to price and quantity. Fewer choices mean less bargaining power to the consumer.

Pursesuitz

Some might view Pursesuitz as very unique or just another option for carrying essential items. If one sees Pursesuitz as a solution to attaining a hands-free lifestyle when out and about, Pursesuitz offers a unique option. If a consumer sees Pursesuitz as just another option to carry essential items, however, then it competes with purses, fanny packs, or backpacks. Branding will be critical in getting consumers to believe Pursesuitz is more than just an alternative to carrying a bag; it is a statement and more comfortable, versatile option.

Center for Health and Wellness Law

There are not a lot of choices for wellness lawyers. I have been told by many people that when searching the Internet for a wellness lawyer, my firm and a firm based in California are the only two results. Thus, if a consumer really wants and needs a lawyer who understands the health and wellness industry, there are not a lot of options in the current market.

4. The Threat of New Entrants

This force looks at how easy or difficult it is for others to enter the market and compete with you. If it is easy, then it will be more challenging for your business to maintain market share. If it is difficult to enter the market, however, then there is a better chance of your business surviving and thriving.

Pursesuitz

I have heard countless times since starting Pursesuitz that "fashion is hard," meaning it has a low barrier to entry. I have a hard time believing that because it takes a lot of work and money to start a fashion business, and not everyone I know has the energy or resources that it takes. But, assuming for sake of argument that fashion does have a low barrier to entry, then I must be prepared for potential competitors of my product or idea. I must face the reality that an established company like Spanx or some other shapewear or athleisure company can easily create pockets in one of its many products, and probably for a lot less investment than I am making as they have established supply chains and can manufacture in high quantities to get the lowest prices, something a start-up like Pursesuitz will not be able to do immediately. Once again, branding and intellectual property protection will be the key to gaining market share and customer loyalty. See Chapter Nine for more about branding.

Center for Health and Wellness Law

The barrier to entry for professional services in general is quite high. First, one has to be a licensed lawyer to practice law, or at least have the credibility of a law degree to give clients confidence that you know what you are talking about. Last I checked, there were only about 1.3 million lawyers in the United States. That is a lot, but you don't need a license or graduate degree to open a fashion business, so there are a lot fewer potential competitors for my law firm. Moreover, not every one of those lawyers are interested in practicing wellness law. There are so many different legal specialties that wellness law is likely not even on the radar of most lawyers. Finally, I have written a book on wellness law, *Rule the Rules of Workplace Wellness Programs*, the first book of its kind. So, anyone who enters the practice area after me will need accept that they will not be the first or the "inventor" of the practice area.

5. The Threat of Substitute Products or Services

One could argue that this fifth force overlaps with the first force: Competitive Rivalry. Nevertheless, this force requires study of how many competitors you have, and comparing the prices and quality of the product or service to your product or service. It also looks at how profitable your competitors are, and whether they could lower their prices even more. This force assumes that consumers would substitute your product or service for a less expensive one if given the opportunity. Again, superior branding will be key to keeping customer loyalty in the face of substitute products or services.

Pursesuitz

Again, depending on how I define the competition, Pursesuitz has very few or many competitors. Looking at the shapewear market only, I am not aware of any shapewear/underwear companies that include functional pockets in their products. That is unique. But it is not the only solution to the problem of where to put essential items. There are companies who make jackets, purses, backpacks, fanny packs, and other items that you put on and take off during the day. But if a woman wants to keep her essential items on her all day without putting something on and taking something off, while having the versatility of wearing the Pursesuitz Pocketwear Tank under dressy or casual clothing, then Pursesuitz is a good solution and thus far, there aren't really any competitors for that.

The question is how big is the market of women who want that type of solution? Again, branding can create a demand where none may not exist currently. Once the demand is there, however, existing shapewear and other athleisure companies can easily jump into the market and become a free rider of the investment that created the interest in the idea. That is a very real risk for Pursesuitz. However, I can combat that risk using intellectual property protections. For example, I can trademark Pursesuitz Pocketwear and patent the design of my hero product. A little investment in intellectual property protection may give me some market advantage, at least for a while.

Center for Health and Wellness Law

There are not many competitors in the wellness law space. There are a lot of lawyers, many of whom claim to be able to help health and wellness clients, but they do not have the depth of expertise in wellness law as my firm. Thus, the health and wellness legal and compliance services my law firm provides are high quality and by national standards, are competitive in price. It is very rare in the legal market for competitors to lower their price. In fact, in many service industries, there is a perception that the higher the cost, the better the service. That is sometimes the case for products as well, particularly if the branding of your product suggests it is a luxury item. But, most shapewear and athleisure clothing lines are not branded as luxury lines like Prada, Chanel, or Hermes, for example.

Putting Them All Together

After you have applied the five forces above for your product or service, put your results in a table like this to see if your product or service has the competitive advantage it needs to be successful and worth your investment of time and money:

Table 7.1
Pursesuitz

Force	Strong Force (Big Worry)	Somewhat Strong (May or May Not be Problematic)	Weak Force (Small to No Worry)
1. Competitive Rivalry		X	
2. Supplier Bargaining Power		X	
3. Customer Bargaining Power		X	
4. Threat of New Entrants	X		
5. Threat of Substitutes		X	

So, based on these results, the potential success of Pursesuitz is up in the air. As I mentioned throughout this exercise, branding will be critical, which is why I am creating my own, new category of clothing called Pursesuitz Pocketwear. By carving out a new category, I automatically limit competition. Moreover, creating a strong brand in advance of, or at the very least in conjunction with the product, will likely make the difference in whether the business succeeds and can gain the attention and loyalty of customers.

Now let's fill in the table for my law firm, the Center for Health and Wellness Law, LLC:

Center for Health and Wellness Law, LLC

Force	Strong Force (Big Worry)	Somewhat Strong (May or May Not be Problematic)	Weak Force (Small to No Worry)
1. Competitive Rivalry			X
2. Supplier Bargaining Power			X
3. Customer Bargaining Power			X
4. Threat of New Entrants			X
5. Threat of Substitutes			X

Compared to Pursesuitz, my law firm is in a very good place, competitively speaking. Marketing and branding is still important, but will not require the same investment as marketing and branding for Pursesuitz will because there is much less competition. Of course, to stay on top of any potential competition, it is vital that my firm's lawyers maintain their knowledge and continue offering thought leadership in the wellness law arena. There is no resting on one's laurels, even if there is not much competition. Clients and customers should always get your best, no matter what.

Filling out this Five Forces table proves to be a very useful exercise in evaluating your competitive position. Here is a blank one for you to fill out for your ambitious idea. If you are trying to climb the corporate ladder, you can use this table to evaluate how your ambitions fare against others who might be aiming for the same promotion or position. For Force Two, suppliers, substitute the number of champions or support people you have. For Force Three, substitute the number of people the ultimate decisionmaker for your promotion or position sees as potential

FIVE FORCES EXERCISE:
Your Ambitious Idea or Goal

Force	Strong Force (Big Worry)	Somewhat Strong (May or May Not be Problematic)	Weak Force (Small to No Worry)
1. Competitive Rivalry			
2. Supplier Bargaining Power			
3. Customer Bargaining Power			
4. Threat of New Entrants			
5. Threat of Substitutes			

No matter where your force evaluation lands, don't get discouraged or overconfident. This is a mere tool to help you see the competitive landscape and plan accordingly. If you find yourself with a lot of X's in the Strong Force category, it is not necessarily a message to give up on your ambitious idea or goal. It just means you need to adjust your timeline and build more momentum before fully launching your idea or next move toward your goal. I firmly believe that nothing is impossible. Circumstances may require you to pivot in ways you did not anticipate until you do the hard work of examining your ideal or goal in the existing landscape.

CHAPTER EIGHT

PROOF OF CONCEPT: WHERE THE RUBBER TRULY MEETS THE ROAD

xxx

BACK IN CHAPTER FIVE, I MENTIONED how lenders and investors want to know the likelihood that your business will be a success. This need for proof places the new entrepreneur in an illogical situation: you need money to prove your concept, but investors want proof before they give you money. Although this proof-of-concept stage can almost seem offensive and can really stretch your budget, it may be one of the most pivotal moments in launching your business.

Fortunately, there are ways you can demonstrate likelihood of success before fully launching your business. Here are some ideas to test the viability of your product or service before producing numerous products or selling your products or services to the masses:

- Focus Groups
- Surveys
- Product testers
- Small production run
- Sample or test service
- Crowdfunding campaigns

We already discussed the value of crowdfunding in Chapter Five. Again, that is a great option for product-based businesses that need to see if their idea can gain traction in the marketplace.

For either service-based or product-based businesses, trying out your service or product on a few friends or family members may provide valuable insight into the viability of your idea. There should be no shame in offering your product or service for free in exchange for objective feedback from your first few "customers." That is what Sara Blakely did with her initial Spanx products. She gave people free product in exchange for wearing her products for a few days so they could give her honest feedback on how the product felt and performed over a few days and in a variety of situations. Such feedback is priceless, and can help you refine your idea before fully launching your business.

Focus groups and surveys are another useful way to get feedback about your idea. For Pursesuitz, I conducted focus groups. Once I had a prototype, I hired a consultant to conduct three focus groups of women from my target audience. These focus groups occurred in different areas of the country. The women could try on the prototype and give honest feedback (since I wasn't there to persuade them for positive feedback only). The focus groups certainly provided valuable, and surprising feedback. Not everyone was a fan of the fabric. They thought the pockets were too high. They didn't like the color choices. They also thought my proposed price point might be too high. Overall, they loved the concept, but thought it might be better suited for travel or leisure rather than work.

I must be honest, hearing this feedback was hard. I had poured so much of my money and self into getting the prototypes developed that I was certain that everyone would be raving about my idea. I was wrong. I had to lick my wounds and re-evaluate. I once heard someone say that through experiencing pain, we learn life's most valuable lessons. The painful criticism about Pursesuitz caused me to stop in my tracks and look around. I had been barreling ahead with my idea that I failed to stop and consider what I had, what I was giving up, and what was important to me. Yes, I believed in my idea, but the focus group feedback forced me to ask myself at what point was my idea no longer worth pursuing? Had I reached it? Did I have the energy and desire to rework my original concept to satisfy the criticisms from the focus group, or should I just give up and be grateful for how far I have come and for what I still had?

The answer for me was to scale back. Instead of doing two layers, I decided to focus on the inner layer and get it right. Scaling back would also save me money, and allow me to price the product at a more accessible amount. Finally, with just one design, instead of multiple designs, I could free up some of my time to refocus on my law firm and my writing. Curiously, while I was diving into Pursesuitz, my law firm did not slow down. In fact, it grew. And Lemonspark, my original entrepreneurial idea that had been on the back burner and for which I had done nothing for years, kept getting "likes" on social media. The painful criticism I experienced with Pursesuitz opened my eyes to what was really resonating with people, which was the Pocketwear Tank, my law firm, and Lemonspark. There is no failure in that.

Thus, the proof-of-concept stage, which you need for investors, is truly the test you must pass to move your idea forward. Not only for the investors, but for you. Once you see your idea come to life and test it in the marketplace, even with just a small group of people, that is when your motivation and rationale for your idea is tested. Depending on what you learn, you may either move forward as planned, or you may need to recalibrate. See Chapter Twelve about next steps. In either case, the information you learn at the proof-of-concept stage is priceless.

CHAPTER NINE:
FIND YOUR BRAND

YOUR BRAND IS YOUR IDENTITY AND your key to success, especially in a crowded market. At least that is what I am observing as I move Pursesuitz along the entrepreneurial process. The fashion market is very crowded, so to stand out from the crowd, your brand must be unique and magnetic. That's easier said than done, I know. But it is not impossible. So how do you tap into your identity to make your brand successful?

By the way, finding your brand applies equally to the entrepreneur as it does to someone trying to climb the corporate ladder. Getting to the top of a company or industry requires fighting a crowded field. In either situation, you need to stand out. Your brand is what helps you stand out.

Find Your Identity

First, note that I said "tap into," not "create." I believe each of us already has a unique identity. Our natural identity. But sometimes that identity gets muffled, hidden, or suppressed. To find your brand, you first need to embrace who you are.

Sara Blakely, founder of Spanx, said in her Masterclass that she was a comedian. She actually did stand-up comedy before Spanx became a success. She used that comedic persona when selling her product. It came out when she appeared at retail stores or on TV. I bet people were drawn to that funny person, and thus drawn to her product. Her identity as a funny, charming person flowed through to her business. That identity of being comical also comes out in her marketing, which unabashedly points out female body flaws and aspirations, such as improving your "butt." To be that direct with language is unique in the market, and I am betting it stems from Sara's comedic roots.

Now I know that I am not a comedian. I appreciate comedy, and I used to think I was funny, but it is not something I have developed and so it is not a strong trait, at least currently. I can, however, write. As a lawyer, I've written a lot. It has not been fiction or fantasy writing, but it's is still good writing. I also can teach. I have been told that I can explain difficult concepts with ease and in a way that most people can understand. One person even told me that my talks on wellness law were like a "School House Rock" series, like explaining how a bill becomes law. That was quite the compliment.

Therefore, to help my brand, I should capitalize on those traits: speaking and writing. I guess I am doing the writing part with this book. My plan is to speak about entrepreneurism and Pursesuitz once the book is published. By speaking and writing about Pursesuitz and becoming an entrepreneur, I am using my identity to build my brand.

Perfect Self-Expression

Another way to look at your identity is what Florence Scovel Shinn calls your perfect self-expression. Perfect self-expression is part of the "square of life," which brings perfect happiness. The other parts of the square of life are health, wealth, and love. According to Florence Scovel Shinn, perfect self-expression will never be labor, but of such absorbing interest that it will seem like play.[35] Fear often stands between you and your perfect self-expression.

"Q" and "r" Factors

Another way of describing your perfect self-expression is what author and scientist Albert-Laszlo Barabawsi calls the "Q" factor.[36] One's "Q" factor is the ability to execute an idea. If you are really passionate about

---

[35] Florence Scovel Shinn, *The Game of Life and How to Play It*, at 76.

[36] Albert-Laszlo Barabawsi, What can we learn from people who succeed later in life?, TED.com (Dec. 11, 2018), available at https://ideas.ted.com/what-can-we-learn-from-people-who-succeed-later-in-life/ (last visited Aug. 8, 2020).

something, your Q factor will likely shine. Your true self will be apparent and your idea or goal has a greater chance of succeeding.

Your idea is the "r" factor. A great idea (a high "r" factor) can still fail if the person executing it is not a good fit for the idea. In other words, you can have a great idea, but if executing it does not bring out your perfect self-expression or "Q" factor, there is a good chance your idea will fail.

The flip side is also true. A person with a strong "Q" factor trying to implement a mediocre idea will face a stronger likelihood of failure.

When both the Q and r factors are strong, however, success is very likely. The formula for this predictor of success is:

$$Q * r = S$$

If you are not displaying your perfect self-expression, you Q factor is likely low. What do you do if you have a low Q factor? Well, according to Barabawsi, a low Q factor probably means you are not breaking through to where you want to be (i.e., your vision, true purpose or as Florence Scovel Shinn describes it, your Divine Design). You are probably chasing after the wrong idea or are in the wrong job.

Q Factor and Social Media

Another more modern measure of whether your Q factor is high or whether you are displaying your perfect self-expression—though I don't really put a lot of stock in this one—is how many social media followers you have. Do your posts attract attention? If they do, that is a good sign you are operating at a high Q factor.

But don't let social media followers or impact be the only measure. You must put that measure into context. I am not saying that if you are operating at a high Q factor, you will overnight have thousands of followers on social media. You might, but that is not the point. The point of operating at a high Q factor is how you feel. If, as Florence Scovel Shinn says, you don't perceive what you do as labor, but more like play, or it brings you joy, the social media presence or impact will likely follow soon thereafter. And if it doesn't, you won't care. In fact, I think social media impact is a better measure than the number of followers. If the quality of your followers is high—that is they believe in what you are trying to accomplish and appreciate your efforts—that is better than having tons of followers who really don't care about you or your goals.

Your Brand is for Your Tribe

As Seth Godin, American author, entrepreneur, and teacher (sethgodin.com) says in his TED Talk "The Tribes We Lead," your entrepreneurial mission is to find and serve your tribe.[37] You or your idea don't need to appeal to everyone, just your "tribe." Your tribe will appreciate your "Q" and "r" factors much more than the general population. Thus, in the end, your brand is about whether you are improving the lives of the members of your tribe. If your idea is able to do that while bringing you joy, then you are likely engaging in your perfect self-expression.

I think that a lot of entrepreneurial success depends on finding your tribe. They are waiting for us to show up with our idea. When I started out with Pursesuitz and began writing this book, I didn't really think about my tribe. Instead, I thought about all professional women. That is a really big tribe. When I did my focus groups of a representative sample of professional women, I discovered that although most liked the idea in theory, none of them were "waiting" for my idea. They were managing just fine without my idea.

There was, however, a fraction of focus group attendees who were just like me, who hated carrying a purse. Those individuals are my tribe. My "Q" factor, which justifies why I am qualified to execute the idea, will shine with other women who, just like me, dislike purses and long to be hands-free. I have firsthand experience with the benefits of my idea, and

---

[37] Seth Godin, TED Talk, The Tribes We Lead (March 3, 2013), available at https://www.youtube.com/watch?v=589tH-wtCak (last visited August 14, 2020).

that will come through when I'm talking about Pursesuitz. My tribe is more likely to embrace my idea and tell others about it. The number of members of my tribe may be far fewer than all professional women (my original "tribe"), but they are the ones whose lives may improve because of my efforts. Knowing that, and scaling Pursesuitz back to focus on my tribe, has been tremendously helpful in mapping out how to move forward.

I had a much easier time defining my tribe for the Center for Health and Wellness Law. When I started my law firm, I had just finished reading a book for lawyers about successful marketing. That book suggested that you find a niche practice area and become one of the few experts in that area. Your niche might be geographic, or it might be subject matter. For me, it was subject matter.

Market research revealed to me that there were not many lawyers in the United States practicing wellness law. In fact, "wellness law" wasn't even a recognized legal practice area. A Google search for "wellness law" typically reveals articles about wellness activities in law firms or police departments, not a legal sub-specialty. Nevertheless, the wellness industry is enormous, encompassing potential clients from individual practitioners (such as healthcare providers and health coaches) to companies that develop wellness products like Fitbits, nutritional supplements, and wellness apps or platforms.

It was shocking to me that other lawyers weren't specializing in servicing that industry. Well, I did find one other lawyer who was specializing in wellness law, and we have since teamed up. But other than the two of us, no other lawyers in the United States have committed their professional lives to serving and helping the wellness industry. So, my tribe for the Center for Health and Wellness Law are those individuals and companies that provide health and wellness services. I am their "go-to" legal resource, and I am quite happy about that.

For Lemonspark, my tribe is also very defined. It is for two tribes of individuals, actually. First, Lemonspark is for those individuals who have recently experienced a lemon in their life. The second group is for people who have moved past their lemon and implemented an idea because of that lemon. The second tribe has an inspiring, helpful, and hopeful story to share with the first tribe. Those Lemonspark stories form the three pillars of Lemonspark's mission:

- To Inspire
- To Give Hope
- To Create a Sense of Belonging

My ability to execute Lemonspark stems from experiencing my own "lemons." Indeed, one of my first real lemons is what sparked the idea for Lemonspark. That lemon was related to a very painful divorce that followed a very difficult infertility journey. During my struggle with infertility, I had a hard time believing I could feel more mental anguish. But, I did. As soon as my twins were born, my husband of ten years left me for another woman whom he got pregnant while I was pregnant with our twins.

For me, that was a new low, the likes of which I had never experienced before. I felt alone, depressed, and confused about why it had all happened. Out of my despair, however, I created Lemonspark as a way to navigate my way through that most challenging time. It gave me power and purpose, and I believed then, as I still believe over fifteen years later, that entrepreneurship is an exit strategy out of what seems like an endless tunnel of agony.

Now that I have described for you three different ideas ("r" factors), I'd like to do an exercise for those of you who may be struggling with finding your right "r" to match your "Q" factor so that you can find the most successful brand on which to focus your efforts. So far, we've learned that your brand consists of two intertwined components:

- You (your "Q" factor)
- Your product or service (the "r" factor)

To find your brand, let's examine your "Q" factor. For each of your ideas or ambitions, ask yourself these questions:

- What traits do you possess that make you extra-qualified to execute your idea? Write down adjectives that describe you, as well as your experience or passion related to each of your ideas.
- Are you committed?
- Are you willing to take risks?
- Does your idea excite you?
- Do you have a clear vision about how your idea will make life better for someone?
- Are you able and willing to talk about and promote your idea?
- Do you have unique experience or education or an interesting story to tell about your idea?

Write your self-description here:

_____

_____

_____

_____

_____

_____

_____

_____

_____

_____

For the purpose of showing examples, here are descriptions for each of my three business ideas:

Pursesuitz:

- I am a woman who detests carrying a purse most of the time.

- I have encountered situations where purses have been an annoyance and a safety risk.

- I have a vision to solve the problem of carrying a purse, based on my experience of using a running belt.

- I have ideas on how to talk about my product and show its usefulness.

- I am willing to put myself out there to record videos, write blogs, and be photographed wearing and using the product.

Center for Health and Wellness Law, LLC

- I have a master's degree in Public Health and a law degree that creates a valuable educational background for wellness law.

- I have long been interested in occupational wellness, an interest that predates my formal education in it.

- I had the desire and ambition to write a book about wellness law.

- I speak and write frequently (at least once per month) about wellness laws.

- I was willing to invest in attending wellness conferences and pick up the phone to meet people in the wellness industry.

Lemonspark

- I experienced two back-to-back lemons in my life, which heightened my ability to empathize with others who experience traumatic events.

- I became obsessed with the question " *Why did this happen to me?* " and sought to find an answer.

- I became aware of the loneliness that often accompanies trauma and the pros and cons of support groups.

- I saw a problem in support groups I attended as focusing only on discussing the traumatic event and not enough on stories of hope.

- I realized that at some point, people need a path to move forward and stories of inspiration can help. I know that I craved to hear those kinds of stories.

- With new technology platforms such as social media and podcasts, there are more options to share those stories.

- I am excited to find those stories and help share them with the individuals who like me, are craving to hear them.

Putting It Together

Once you have written down your "Q" factor lists, examine them and the process closely. If you have a single ambition or idea, determine whether you are satisfied with your uniqueness to execute your idea. If not, is there something you can do to make you stand out more? To make you more convincing? Can you take a class, certificate program, or write an article or book to bolster your uniqueness? Or perhaps you could conduct more research, such as a survey, to give you more inside knowledge. Or maybe as you wrote your list, you realized that you struggled to come up with descriptions that make you uniquely qualified to implement your idea. Does the struggle suggest a lack of passion, commitment or vision?

If you have more than one ambition or idea, were some lists easier to write than others? Maybe the ease with which you wrote your list is telling you where to focus your efforts. I'm not suggesting that you give up, but maybe the process is pointing you toward a need to recalibrate or re-scale your idea. For your "r" factor to succeed, your "Q" factor or brand must be strong and convincing.

CHAPTER TEN
FIND YOUR TEAM

AT SOME POINT DURING YOUR entrepreneurial journey, you will inevitably search for help from others. This may be in the form of mentors or champions, which we discussed in Chapter Two, or people you hire to help you with aspects of your venture that you are unable to learn or do yourself. When looking for funding, potential funders will evaluate your competence and ability to succeed. Your competence and ability could come from your own knowledge and skills, but it could also derive from your team members. People you hire to build your website, manage your social media, create your proof of concept, market your idea, or protect your idea can all be part of your team. It is imperative to find team members you trust.

So how do you find people with the skills you can trust? Here are some ideas.

Entrepreneur Groups
One way I found some good team members was through joining a women's entrepreneur group. The group's leaders and members recommended people who could develop websites, as well as provide marketing and social media services. If I wanted to use the group to find trustworthy and affordable accountants, lenders, lawyers and others, members would likely have recommendations for those as well. There are many entrepreneur groups, however, that you can join to not only learn about creating a business plan and other entrepreneurial infor-mation, but also to make essential connections.

Business Plan Contests

If you are fortunate to participate in a business plan contest, such contests also offer a great way to get mentorship from fellow business owners and professionals. In addition to monetary awards, these contests also offer help in building your business through essential business services, such as marketing and branding. Through those contests, you are likely to meet some potential team members.

Networking

Another way to find team members is just by talking to people about your idea. That is how I found my business consultant and fashion designer for Pursesuitz. Recall in Chapter Three, we discussed that one of the key actions you can do to help your idea succeed is to start talking about it. Not only does verbalizing your idea help refine your idea and solidify your commitment to it, it also gives those who learn about your idea the opportunity to connect you with others who may be able to help. My neighbor was the person who connected me with my business consultant, and I found my fashion designer by cold-calling various clothing manufacturers (that I found through Google searches).

Other Entrepreneurs

When I started my law firm, one of the first things a fellow entrepreneur told me was that other entrepreneurs would flock to new entrepreneurs to help them. Entrepreneurs are mostly a community of like-minded individuals who want to help others succeed.

That early piece of wisdom was mostly true. I did find a willingness on the part of other entrepreneurs to talk to me and give me suggestions about how to move forward. This was especially true for fellow attorneys who had struck out on their own. Through their suggestions, I found my law firm's accountant and web developer. By talking about my law firm at continuing legal education events, I found other attorneys who were interested in working with me. I am so grateful for these connections and most of those connections are still part of my law firm's team today.

Advisory Board

I initially created Lemonspark as a nonprofit organization, which by law must have a board of directors with a president, secretary, and treasurer. A nonprofit board must meet at least once per year and the secretary must take minutes at each meeting.

After several meetings, I began to realize the value of having a board of directors. Boards that are diverse in terms of age, race, gender, profession, and income can bring incredible perspective and ideas to an organization.

Lemonspark's initial board brought valuable insight to my idea, and helped shape it in its very early existence. Eventually, because I decided to put the idea on my backburner, Lemonspark's nonprofit status expired and the board disbanded. However, as I work to revive Lemonspark, I recall the value of having a board of advisors.

For any idea, whether it is a product or service, an effective way to find trusted help is to create an advisory board. The board may consist of friends, acquaintances, or champions who want to see you succeed. Each of these advisors can lead you to other team members to help your idea succeed.

Asking people to be on your advisory board is not as challenging as it may sound. You might be surprised how willingly some talented people will give their time to be part of a new venture. Some advisors may want to financially invest in your venture as well, but that is absolutely not necessary. For some entrepreneurs, it may not even be preferred. Offering insight and advice is extremely valuable. In addition, an advisory board can serve as a built-in focus group to test out new ideas before spending a lot of resources to bring the idea to market.

A Word About Employees vs. Independent Contractors

Once you find your team members, you can use their unique skills and perspectives to refine and improve your idea. Formal and informal advisors can offer valuable insight, but in the end, it is your choice whether or not to accept that advice. Other team members, such as product designers or marketing/social media professionals you may consider employing. I think a lot of business owners make the mistaken assumption that they need to employ team members rather than considering the possibility of hiring independent contractors. This is especially the case if your team members are expert in a subject area that you are not.

> **Practical Tip**
> Have an independent contractor agreement with your consultant team members that spells out what you are responsible for (timely payment and responses to questions) and what the independent contractor is responsible for (own insurance, benefits, taxes, equipment, timely responses and services, etc.).

Independent contractors are individuals who do work for you, typically using their own judgment as to what needs to be done. You as the business owner just tell them what you need done, and they set about getting it done using their skill set.

For example, I hired a fashion designer for Pursesuitz, as I know nothing about fashion design. I just had the idea for pockets in a blouse. My husband, who sews, created the first prototype and gave me hope that this idea might just work. Then I described my idea to a fashion designer and she drew the concept and worked with the seamstress to create the pattern and second prototype. Even though I consider my fashion designer a part of my team, I didn't hire her as an employee. I paid her as an independent contractor consultant.

Unlike employees, independent contractors have their own business and thus are responsible for paying their own taxes and benefits. As the business owner you pay for their skills as needed, but you don't need to worry about making payroll each month if business is slow. The independent contractor obtains and pays for their own equipment, benefits, employment taxes, insurance and whatever else they need to provide their services. But, they also have the freedom to work for as many clients they want, not just for you.

From a legal perspective, it is very important to keep control over what the independent contractor does in the hands of the independent contractor. The more control you try to exert over the independent contractor, especially in terms of when they work and how they work, the more likely the government will deem them an employee. If that happens, you as the business owner may be responsible for paying loads of back taxes on that independent contractor-now-turned-employee.

CHAPTER ELEVEN

SELL YOUR IDEA

ONCE YOU SETTLE ON YOUR IDEA, who it's for, your ability and desire to execute it, and have a satisfactory proof of concept, it's time to start selling it. Getting the word out about your idea is how you get business. To be successful, however you define success, you need your target customers to buy into your idea. To do that, you need to market. This chapter will explore the different ways you can market your idea so that it gains traction and has the impact you set out to make.

Social Media

Whether you are selling a product or service, most potential customers expect to see and learn about your idea on social media. Depending on what you are selling and who you are selling it to, some social media channels will be more effective than others. Many consumer products do well on Instagram and Facebook, and even Pinterest. That is why I am targeting those social media sites when marketing Pursesuitz. Wellness and coaching services also seem to do well on Facebook and Instagram.

For professional services and products, LinkedIn is a must. I'm beginning to believe Facebook is also a must for professional services, even though I did not believe that was the case just a year ago. I've had a Facebook page for my law firm since the beginning, but I didn't think many potential clients found my firm through that medium. Over the last year, however, I have seen an uptick in the number of page likes and followers for my law firm. I believe this is because a lot of my clients and potential clients promote their products and services on Facebook and Instagram, and so they spend a lot of time on those sites. Therefore, if your target consumer likely spends a lot of time on a social media site, I suggest promoting your idea on that site.

Jennifer Abernethy, owner and founder of Socially Delivered, a social media promotion company, has this advice for maximizing impact on social media: [38]

❏ Think of yourself as a brand, even if you are representing a company (not your own).

❏ Get comfortable with video. People gravitate toward videos and they are getting easier to make with your phone's camera.

❏ Start connecting to people outside of your industry. Expanding your network to others who are not in the same line of work for you helps you build more meaningful connections to help others and possibly builds a referral network for your product or service. This includes attending a conference outside of your industry at least once per year to help build those referral connections and stand out from the crowd.

❏ Be active on as many social media channels as possible.

❏ Write personal notes on LinkedIn when connecting with other members. Base your personal note on their profile. This makes the connection more meaningful for you and them.

❏ Get an updated headshot and use it on social media.

Write a Book

I'm a big fan of writing books. I view authorship as a gateway to almost all the other types of marketing discussed below.

In addition to this book, I have written *Rule the Rules on Workplace Wellness Programs.* The process and the ultimate product are endless sources of knowledge and material to repurpose for marketing. Writing a book often requires some research so you can provide more valuable information to your reader. Doing the research and then putting that research into your own words is highly educational. That is why authors seem so smart when they talk about their books. They have spent countless hours thinking, reading and writing about the topics

---

[38] Phone Interview with Jennifer Abernethy of Socially Delivered (March 16, 2020).

discussed in the book. That is also why authors are often asked to speak at conferences, and can charge money for speaking at conferences. They also get the bonus of selling copies of their books at conferences, which many publishers count on when determining whether they want to publish your book. I was told by one publishing agent that particularly for self-help books, big-name publishers expect to make most of their money on selling books at conferences at which the author speaks.

During COVID-19, when in-person conferences all but disappeared, the publishing of self-help books by major publishers also became less attractive. Nevertheless, I believe with the advent of virtual conferences, there may be ways for authors to continue speaking and promoting their books. We just have to think a bit more creatively, such as providing links to attendees to order our books online and receiving a special discount if they order within a certain time period after our presentation.

A valuable benefit of writing a book is the almost endless fountain of written material that you can repurpose as blog posts and articles. These blogs or articles can provide snippets of useful information that the reader can explore more by purchasing your book. In essence, your book can become a menu of "teaser" material.

Finally, arguably the most valuable aspect to writing a book is the credibility it establishes for your reputation and business. As noted above, the process of writing a book somewhat automatically makes you an expert. That is why it may become easier to secure speaking engagements. For your business, whether it offers a service or a product, there is something more impressive about buying a product or service from the author of a published book. You can showcase your book on your business's website and social media pages, which of course helps promote book sales as well as give your business some extra cachet.

Publishing Options: Self-Publishing, Traditional Publishing, or Hybrid Publishing

There are so many options now for writing and publishing a book. You can self-publish, or find a publisher willing to publish your book for you. There are also hybrid options, where you as the author invest some money in publishing your book and a publisher helps you edit, print, market, and distribute your book. I have looked into hybrid publishing and the upfront investment ranges from $1,500 to $50,000. For most people, that amount, especially the larger amounts, is not practical or doable. Unless you can charge $10,000 or more per speaking engagement to promote your book, I think you will have a hard time recouping that cost. True, you may get a higher percentage of sales and access to national booksellers, but given all the other option available, you can find a publishing route that is the right fit for you.

Traditional publishers don't ask you to invest any money, and many of the big-name publishers cut you a check to write your book, called an "advance on royalties." They also are connected with the large booksellers, so your book has a good chance of being sold through national bookstores, as well as online. The tradeoff is that you get a lower percentage of book sales. Depending on the publisher, you may be able to negotiate a higher percent of the sales, or royalties. It is definitely worth trying to do.

Of course, if you self-publish, then you get 100 percent of the sales. But you have no one helping you edit, print, and market your book. I have a colleague who is self-publishing a law book, and it is a grueling process. She is spending so much time and money on editing, formatting the text, book cover design, cite checking sources of law, and so on. In the end, she will have produced an incredibly valuable resource, but way behind her initial schedule. Once she has her book printed and ready for sale, then she is solely responsible for marketing and promoting it, which will cost even more money and time. Luckily, she has a very targeted market for her book and is well connected within that market already, so she will likely have an easier time getting the word out about the book than someone without all those connections.

How Do I Find a Publisher?

You can find a publisher on your own, or find a literary agent who can hunt for a publisher for you. I simply searched Google for publishers. A lot of publishers list the types of books they are seeking to publish. Some specialize in self-help books, others religious books, and others fiction books. Working through an agent means the agent gets a cut of what you get paid (usually 15 percent of royalties, according to Jane Friedman, author of *How to Find a Literary Agent for your Book*).[39] However, Jane Friedman also states that about 80 percent of books published by New York publishing houses are sold through literary agents.[40] Two good resources for finding literary agents and learning more about what major publishing houses look for in a manuscript are these two websites:

> https://agentquery.com/publishing_mp.aspx
> https://www.publishersmarketplace.com/

There are also a lot of smaller publishers outside of New York and if you are writing a book for a niche market, or an academic book, then you probably don't need a literary agent. And seriously, if you don't plan on writing a *New York Times* bestseller aiming to sell over 10,000 copies, you really should just start with the smaller publishing houses. The point of your book is ultimately to enhance your credibility and business, not necessarily become the next JK Rowling (though that would be nice). I don't mean to lower your expectations, however. If you really believe your book idea has the potential of the same success as the next Harry Potter series, then by all means aim high and find a literary agent. If you are not aiming to write that next blockbuster book, however, here is a website where you can find a list of smaller, independent publishers:

---

[39] Jane Friedman, How to find a literary agent for your book, Dec. 5, 2017, available at https://www.janefriedman.com/find-literary-agent/ (last visited August 21, 2020).
[40] Ibid.

https://medium.com/the-nonconformist/the-big-big-list-of-indie-publishers-and-small-presses-5e83e9522b5c

For my *Rule the Rules for Workplace Wellness Programs* book, I used the American Bar Association press because they specialize in publishing legal books. For this book, I am working with HenschelHAUS Publishing, a Wisconsin-based publisher, and I couldn't be happier. Henschel-HAUS offers both hybrid and traditional publishing options.

What Should You Write About?
Ideally, for purposes of connecting your business with your book, you should aim to write about something that ties back to your entrepreneurial idea. Maybe it's a story of how you developed your idea, or maybe your book describes the importance of your idea. Perhaps the description is a historical explanation that is the basis your idea, or how your idea solves a modern-day problem.

If you are a service-based entrepreneur, you could write a self-help book aimed at either your prospective clients or fellow service providers. Or, perhaps you do a deep dive into one aspect of your service and write the defining book for that topic. That is how I view *Rule the Rules of Workplace Wellness Programs;* it is the only book about which I am aware on workplace wellness laws. And, that book brought me a lot of credibility and speaking opportunities for my law firm business.

Whatever you decide to write about, be patient and persistent. Write at a designated time each day and you will slowly find yourself the author of a book.

Write Blogs and Articles
Even if you don't write a book, another great way to market is to write blogs and articles that draw attention to your brand and your business. This was one of the primary marketing methods I learned while working in Big Law. Because lawyers sell their knowledge, an obvious way to

showcase that knowledge is to write and speak about what you know. The same is true for any other type of business.

What really helps with writing about your brand and business is to have an underlying mission or cause to your business. That gives you much more material to write about. For example, for Pursesuitz, I wanted the company mission to be about gender equality and hands-free convenience. Pursesuitz aims to include pockets in women's clothes to address the gender discriminatory history behind the absence of pockets in female clothing. With this gender equality mission, I can write not only for fashion magazines, but also professional women's publications. The topics I can write about include the history behind women's clothing, gender inequality in the workplace and in the community, as well as living a carefree lifestyle for wellness publications.

For my law firm, my mission is to help the health and wellness industries with compliance issues. I can write about various compliance issues for the numerous national health and wellness publications that exist, as well as for publications by health and wellness associations. Indeed, I have an arrangement to write a monthly blog post for the Wellness Councils of America, which has been extremely helpful in raising awareness about my law firm among the workplace wellness community.

For Lemonspark, I can also write for wellness and psychology publications about the power of stories from people who have experienced trauma and turned it into something beneficial.

Writing for national publications or blog platforms such as *Medium*, *Vox*, or the *Huffington Post*, as examples, introduces your brand and business to multitudes of readers. In your byline for the publication, you can link to your website and social media sites. Here are examples for each of my ventures:

Pursesuitz:
Barbara J. Zabawa is author of *The Tug* and founder of Pursesuitz, maker of convenient and hands-free fashion that also promotes gender

equality. Learn more at www.pursesuitz.com. Follow her on Instagram @pursesuitz and on Facebook at www.facebook.com/pursesuitz.

Center for Health and Wellness Law, LLC:

Barbara J. Zabawa is author of *Rule the Rules of Workplace Wellness Programs* and founder of the Center for Health and Wellness Law, LLC, a law firm dedicated to helping the health and wellness industries stay protected and compliant. Contact her at bzabawa@wellnesslaw.com and learn more at www.wellnesslaw.com. You can follow her on Twitter @wellnessatty, LinkedIn www.linkedin.com/in/barbarazabawa, Instagram wellnessattorney, and Facebook @centerforhealthandwellnesslaw.

Lemonspark:

Barbara J. Zabawa is founder of Lemonspark, a podcast featuring stories of hope, inspiration, and community from people who have experienced traumatic events that sparked a new way forward. Learn more at www.lemonspark.com and follow her on Instagram @lemonsparkstories and Facebook at www.facebook.com/lemonspark.

To learn more about how to write effective articles and become a regular writer for national publications, I strongly suggest enrolling in Susie Moore's course *Five Minutes to Famous*. I learned a lot of helpful tips on getting published in national publications that are directed toward a variety of niche markets. You can find out more about Susie Moore's course and educational materials at www.fiveminutestofamous.com.

Instead of or in addition to writing a blog, you can always do a short, one-minute vlog (a video blog). With smart phones, these are easier than ever to do. Just point the camera toward you and give a brief summary of the topic. Give one or two pointers to your audience and then upload the video to social media channels. According to one social media expert, Jennifer Abernethy of Socially Delivered, short videos generally get a lot more attention than written material. Plus, if someone likes what you say in your video, at your strategic suggestion, they can always learn more by going to your website to read the full article or blog.

Speak

A natural companion to writing either a book or articles is public speaking. Since you have written material on a topic you have researched, turning that information into an oral presentation should not be too difficult. Many of the same organizations and interest areas that sponsor publications also sponsor conferences. Conference planners are always looking for fresh faces and topics for presentation slots. Again, Google is a great resource to find conferences and meetings that happen annually. Research those websites and learn how and when to submit speaker proposals. Many times, proposals are due over six months before the event, so plan accordingly. Being able to cite to a written product, such as a book or article, will help you stand out from the crowd of submissions.

Once you are approved to speak at a conference, use the event strategically. Announce on social media that you will be speaking at the event, and tag the event as a hashtag to your post. Thank the conference sponsors and tag them in your post. The more people and organizations you can tag, the more likely your post will be shared with others. The more shares, the more visibility you have. If more people see you, there is a good chance they will also see your business.

At the event, if you are able and not in violation of any speaker agreement, mention your business (and book, if you have one). Make sure the last slide in your presentation deck lists your website and all of your social media handles and encourage attendees to follow you on social media.

It is beyond the focus of this book to instruct you on effective presentations. There are plenty of resources for learning how to create and deliver memorable presentations. Joining a local Toastmaster's club is another good way to practice public speaking. I have thought about doing that many times. Needless to say, effective public speaking is a skill I am still trying to master. I do know, however, that presentation slides should not be too wordy, you shouldn't read from your slides, and humor and stories are always good to include where possible.

Volunteer for Key Organizations

Volunteering for an organization that serves your potential customers or potential referral sources is an effective way to get name recognition in your industry, as well as to deepen your skills. Volunteering may include helping out with an event (such as planning or staffing the event), writing for one of the organization's publications, or serving on a committee or board of directors for that organization.

Serving as a board member for an organization that supports and serves your clientele offers many opportunities to network with people who can be keys to your business's success. Board members learn about industry trends and meet individuals who are interested in the same niche market. You can learn a lot from your fellow board members, as well as the employees of the organization. You can also offer your knowledge to fellow board members, as well as the clientele of the organization, either through helping on projects or writing for the organization's publication. If the organization holds annual events, you are expected to attend the event as a board member. Many times you are able to speak at the event as well.

As I mentioned earlier, nonprofit organizations must, by law, have a board of directors. Thus, serving on a nonprofit board is usually an attainable goal. Most nonprofits seek board members who have a certain interest, perspective, or skill set to diversify their board membership. If you are unable to get on a certain board of directors, volunteer for a committee. Many of these organizations have committees comprised of both board and community members. Community members who show interest in board membership through committee work have a good chance of being elected to the board once a seat opens up.

Hiring Social Media Help

If your business is direct-to-consumer, you may be tempted to hire a social media company or influencer to help boost your presence and effectiveness on social media channels. Whether this is money well spent depends on a few factors:

First, are you a novice at social media? If so, you might benefit from the expert help.

Second, do you have the money to spend but not the time to routinely post on social media? If so, then maybe hiring a company to post for you is a good idea, as long as it is producing results. It is really important to make sure any social media help you hire is actually translating to results. Results should be measured in traffic to your website and ultimately, sales of your product or service. If you or they are not tracking that, then you are probably wasting money.

Also, if you plan to hire a social media company or influencer, it is really important that you hire someone whom your potential clients will trust and whether they will be able to reach the right customers for you. The work you did in Chapter Six should help you and your social media helpers find the right messaging, platforms, video content, and images to attract your potential customers and increase your social media and website traffic.

If you don't have a lot of money to spend on marketing and you do have a general idea about how social media works, then make time to make your own posts. You can enlist services that allow you to post once and automatically share that post across several different social media sites, saving you a ton of time. Some social media tools to help automate, create, and schedule your posts include:

- Loomly
- AgoraPulse
- Promo Republic
- Hootsuite
- Buffer
- Sprout Social
- TweetDeck
- SocialOomph

- MeetEdgar
- CoSchedule
- Tailwind
- Everypost
- Sendible
- Crowdfire
- Later

For a good summary of what each of these tools has to offer and access to the individual web links, see https://influencermarketinghub.com/social-media-posting-scheduling-tools/.

Many of these tools have free services, as well as more comprehensive services for a monthly fee. You will need to do the homework to determine which tool is a good fit for your social media needs. I personally use Sendible, which I find incredibly easy to use and efficient.

What if I can't get into an already-existing platform to talk or write about my idea?

As much as I love the prospect of writing for a well-known publication or speaking for a popular organization, it's not always possible for everyone. I have encountered rejection many times. I submit a fantastic article or speaking proposal to a well-established organization, and it is rejected out of hand. Most of the time, I don't even know why.

At that point, you have one of two options. You can keep trying, perhaps branching out to other publications or speaking opportunities. Or, you can create your own platform. You can always feature blogs or articles on your own website. You can create your own podcast or newsletter. You can create a YouTube channel to teach potential clients via video. And there is always social media, where you can feature snippets of your own blogs or videos.

In other words, don't despair.

Get your message out there, no matter what. Who knows? In due time, those rejections might turn into acceptances down the road after people find you because of your content. That has happened to me numerous times. People have read my content and then reached out to me and invited me to blog or speak for their organization. Regardless of which option you choose, don't give up!

Wrapping It Up

As my fashion designer has told me with regard to Pursesuitz, having a fashion brand is 20 percent product and 80 percent marketing (at least in terms of budget). I'm not sure if I completely agree with that percentage split, but sales and marketing certainly are key aspects to a fashion brand's revenue generation.

Note that I didn't say marketing is a key aspect of "success." Success to you may be improving the life of one person. In that case, you don't need a very big marketing budget at all.

If, on the other hand, you seek to impact as many people as possible, you need to raise awareness about your business and brand. This chapter has offered a few examples on how to do that. It is not an exhaustive list, however. We didn't discuss paid advertising in publications, sponsoring or exhibiting at conferences, or radio/television ads. I assume the readers of this book are not looking to do those kinds of marketing activities just yet. What we have focused on is content marketing. For the start-up, I believe content marketing is the most economical and impactful ways to stretch your marketing budget while giving you the exposure you need to reach your version of success.

Chapter Twelve
What's Next? Scale Up, Scale Back, or Embrace the Present

AFTER MARKETING YOUR NEW BUSINESS for several months, you may be able to assess consumer response. In the grand scheme of things, a few months is not a long time, but for the budding entrepreneur, it can feel like an eternity. Depending on the responses (or lack thereof) from consumers, you may have thoughts about what to do next. If you experience a lot of energy around your business idea on social media and website traffic, you might start thinking it's time to scale up. Alternatively, if your marketing efforts seem to be falling on deaf ears, you may wonder whether you should scale back, or heaven forbid, quit altogether. Or, your efforts might bring in just enough business that you feel like you don't need to do anything different.

Regardless, you will reach a point in your entrepreneurial journey about what to do next. Whenever you reach that point, you will have likely invested a lot of time, energy, money, and belief in yourself to get there. It may be that your idea is taking hold with others and you feel validated in your venture. Or, it may be that life has thrown you a curve ball or two and your gut is telling you to hit the "pause" button or just clean up and go home. Or it may be something in between.

I think that "something in between" outcome gets little credit as an option. The truth is, if you really believe in your idea, which we explored extensively in Chapter One, then there is merit to keep going in some form. That may mean scaling back or at least not scaling up, for now. There is no deadline for your business's success except the ones you impose on yourself. You don't have to quit. Instead, you can refocus your effort on something more manageable, and it's ok. Indeed, scaling back instead of quitting may be more palatable because life does happen, and we must adjust sometimes. Scaling back also means your idea doesn't die and doesn't become part of the sad business failure statistics where fifty percent of small businesses fail within the first four years of existence, and only two to three businesses out of ten survive fifteen or more years.[41]

Scaling Back on Lemonspark and Pursesuitz

To give you even more permission that it's ok to scale back on your idea, let me share my thoughts on two of my ventures and why I decided to scale back on them.

Lemonspark

I hit the "pause button" for Lemonspark because the time just wasn't right both for me personally as well as in terms of the means to make it happen efficiently. When I started Lemonspark, I had a lot of positive reaction (before social media was popular). I had no trouble finding Lemonspark stories and getting people to tell them. Those who heard the stories reached out to me and thanked me for sharing the inspiration. I could have scaled up, but I wasn't sure how at the time. And, other priorities in my life took over, so I placed Lemonspark on the back burner until its time was ripe again. I didn't know exactly when that would be or how I would know, but somewhere deep down I fully intended to return to Lemonspark because it was a good idea. I never lost faith in that.

Fast forward about 15 years and Lemonspark seems to be ready to begin anew. Though it has sat dormant for the last ten years or so, it continues to get likes on social media. And, with the advent of podcasts

---

[41]Andrew Deen, Five Signs that it's Time to Scale up Your Business, *Bplans*, available at https://articles.bplans.com/five-signs-that-its-time-to-scale-up-your-business/ (last visited September 5, 2020) (citing Bureau of Labor Statistics 2016 data and Forbes research).

and Zoom, recording interviews and sharing them widely has helped clear the path on how to move forward with Lemonspark. With so many people experiencing trauma, and relatively easy ways to share stories of those who overcame trauma, Lemonspark now has a place to exist and thrive. Plus, now that I am self-employed, I have more flexibility to find and schedule interviews. My kids are also older and don't need me as much as they did ten years ago. So, in the case of Lemonspark, technology and life's circumstances just needed to catch up with my idea, and I feel very optimistic about Lemonspark 2.0.

Pursesuitz

When I started Pursesuitz, I had a big vision of becoming the next Spanx or MM LaFleur. I was fascinated by two women who, like myself, had no experience or formal education in the fashion industry and yet still achieved success by being persistent, creative, and finding the right team members. That sounded like a good roadmap to me, and I felt like I had an endless supply of drive to get me there.

Then I did the focus groups to get feedback on my prototypes, and the response was mixed at best. My expectations and the market expectations didn't seem to match. Specifically, my whole premise about serving primarily professional women was undercut by comments from focus group attendees that they would rather wear the inner tank only and wear it for travel or leisure, not business. Even more surprising to me, however, was the desire the focus group women had for their purses. The majority of focus group attendees loved their purses and couldn't imagine a professional life without it. That was a bitter pill to swallow and thoughts of giving up were surfacing and taking hold.

Then I talked with a dear friend who also happens to have a life coaching business. I can't say enough about the value of finding a life or business coach. Coaches can really help you find clarity of thought when you seem to be swimming in confusion. Anyway, my friend and I spoke a few times about Pursesuitz. I told her that I felt overwhelmed by everything. I had numerous commitments, such as more-than-full-time employment, as well as serving as a board member on several different organizations. Now I was trying to launch Pursesuitz. It was easy to take the criticism from the focus groups as a sign that maybe I should give up before I spent any more money and energy on an idea that wasn't fully resonating with my intended market.

My friend listened to me and then said, "But it's still a good idea." She encouraged me to rethink my original aspirations of becoming the next Spanx and accept that it was ok to scale back. She lasered in on the one or two women in my focus groups who, like me (and her), did not like carrying purses and were looking for options. Those women were my tribe, not all professional women.

Suddenly, the clouds of confusion cleared. In that moment, the path forward made sense and it didn't involve quitting. Instead, I would focus only on the inner layer, lower the pockets, create a prototype in black, and allow women to decide when and how they would want to wear it. By scrapping the outer layer, women now had the option of wearing the inner layer alone, or under whatever type of top they wanted: a t-shirt, sweatshirt, or blouse. Because the pockets were lower, women would not need to lift up the outer layer very much to access the pockets. I could also embroider my logo on the inner layer to give it more flair in case someone wanted to wear it as a standalone piece, such as for athletic reasons. Finally, because I was focusing on the inner layer only, the price point just became more accessible for a lot more women. I renamed the inner layer the "Pocketwear Tank" and that became my hero product.

It was a revelation and relief to scale back. I felt like I could move forward at a more reasonable pace without sacrificing my other commitments. Scaling back instead of giving up felt empowering, and I strongly encourage any of you who are reading this to consider that option as you move forward with your venture, especially if you still believe in your idea.

When Should You Scale Up?

Before you can answer this question, you should first have a pretty good idea of where you want your business to end up. Are you aiming to sell it in five to ten years? Or, is this something you envision doing for the rest of your life to give you enough flexibility and income to work when and where you want? Those are two very different goals.

The first goal probably requires scaling up at some point. The second does not necessarily require significant scaling up, if any at all. Moreover, what it means to scale up can mean different things to different people. It might mean you hire a few independent contractors to fill in during busy times, or it might mean hiring a fleet of employees and expanding your product line. Depending on what scaling up means to you, your strategy will vary. Now would be a good time to write down how you envision the end game of your business:

_____

_____

_____

_____

_____

What if you don't have a clue about where you want your business idea to go? That's ok. As I have learned over the years of being an entrepreneur, sometimes the path forward reveals itself to you. Yes, if you aim to create the next Fortune 500 company, then you need a vision to get there. As Florence Scovel Shinn says (in dated language, of course) "Man can only receive what he sees himself receiving."[42] Your vision will lead you to take the steps needed to get there.

---

[42] Scovel Shinn, p 19.

But if that is not what you are aiming for (or at least you aren't salivating to get there), then I believe it's ok to just start down the entrepreneurial path and see where it leads. Of course, if you need funding from external sources like banks or investors, this "wait and see" approach will not help you obtain funding. No one wants to invest in someone who doesn't have a clear vision of great financial success.

If, however, you have flexibility in your venture, then there really is no need to put pressure on yourself to perform at a certain level. The universe will reveal to you if and when it is time to grow. And as I mentioned earlier, there are multiple ways to grow. Growth doesn't necessarily mean you have to hire traditional "employees" or buy or rent real estate, for example. My expansion of my law firm, the Center for Health and Wellness Law, LLC, offers another example of "growth."

Growing the Center for Health and Wellness Law, LLC

When I established the Center for Health and Wellness Law, LLC, in 2014, I started with just me and my husband. I did the legal work and he learned how to do the financial records. Through a fellow attorney entrepreneur, I found an accountant to help with the books. My state bar association also provided some resources for starting a solo practice.

At the time, I thought I would want and need external office space to practice law, and maybe even a legal secretary. Soon, I realized that was not necessary and just added overhead. So, for the first few years, I just embraced the status quo. I had just enough client work each month to keep going.

After the first three years, however, I had an opportunity to teach at the University of Wisconsin—Milwaukee. My law firm was not slowing down, but I wouldn't have as much time to devote to the legal work, so I hired an independent contractor attorney who has been incredibly helpful. I hired two others recently as well. I know other attorneys who can do legal projects when I am stretched too thin to do them myself. They also bring different skill sets to enhance the types of services my law firm can offer. Since we all work virtually, there is still no need for an office lease. Thus, even though I didn't view it that way in the beginning, my law firm has scaled up.

Signs It is Time to Scale Up

So what are some signals that might be telling you it is time to scale up? According to Andrew Deen from BPlans,[43] here are some cues that it might be time to grow:

- ❏ **You are turning down potential business opportunities.** If your business network is overwhelming your existing workforce and you need to reject projects or orders because you just can't fulfill them, it may be time to expand.

- ❏ **Surpassing your goals.** If you set course to meet a certain goal, either financial or number of orders or clients, and you exceed that goal, then it may be time to up your game and set a new, even higher goal.

- ❏ **Strong cash flow and repeatable sales.** Once you are in business for a while and can accurately forecast revenue and expenses, you will have a pretty good idea of whether you want to stay the course or seek to expand.

- ❏ **Proven concept and reliable infrastructure.** Is your idea selling in the marketplace, and are you and your employees ready for growth? If you and your team are itching to see your idea expand in revenue, product offerings and/or geography, then it may be time to let your team forge ahead with expansion.

- ❏ **An atmosphere of minimal risk.** Are you in a position to expand without having to take on a lot of expense or learning to do it? If so, then that is a good sign that the time is ripe to scale up.

---

[43] Andrew Deen, Five Signs that it's Time to Scale up Your Business, Bplans, available at https://articles.bplans.com/five-signs-that-its-time-to-scale-up-your-business/ (last visited September 5, 2020) (citing Bureau of Labor Statistics 2016 data and Forbes research).

How to Scale Up

Assuming you decide it's time to scale up, here are some methods from *Entrepreneur Magazine* you can use to grow.

❑ Find cash to expand. If you need an infusion of cash to expand your business idea, consider crowdfunding options. It is a lower risk option to see if your expansion idea has legs in the marketplace. Otherwise there are traditional funding options, as discussed in Chapter Five of this book.

❑ Create a new revenue stream. This is an exciting prospect for growing your business. If you have a service-based business, think about whether you can create an educational product as another means to share your knowledge with customers. This might be an educational toolkit, book or compliance toolkit, as examples. I have had clients do this very successfully. For example, if you are a coach, think beyond the one-on-one coaching sessions. Perhaps you could offer paid seminars, group sessions or retreats. If you sell products, think about a creating a complementary product to sell. For example, for Pursesuitz, I thought about creating a cosmetic line that would be compact enough to stick in the pockets of the main product.

❑ Enter into a joint venture. This may be one of the "easiest" ways to expand. If there is another business that either competes with you, or complements your business, it might make sense to align with them. You might combine your businesses into one, or you might refer business to one another. However you seek to join your businesses, make sure you do it legally. Joint ventures have the potential to violate antitrust laws, and if you are in healthcare, fee splitting and other fraud and abuse laws. Having a competent lawyer on your team when you seek this method of growth is essential.[44]

If you aren't sure what method makes sense, or if there may be others, another good option is to seek strategic advice from more seasoned business owners who have the success you want. Meet them virtually, or if you are close enough geographically, for coffee or lunch to pick their brain about what they did to get to the next level.

---

[44] Allen Brouwer and Cathryn Lavery, Tim Ferriss Explains How to Scale your Business in 3 Steps, *Entrepreneur* (Dec. 11, 2017), available at https://www.entrepreneur.com/article/305588 (last visited Sept. 6, 2020).

What's Next?

Embrace the Present

Of course, you might be at a point in your business where everything seems to be "just right," not too big, not too small. That is an enviable position in which to be, so savor it. No one says you must expand or scale back. You could keep offering your products or services at your current level and not have to change a thing, unless you want to. But not everyone wants to. I think this is lost on a lot of aspiring entrepreneurs, as well as outsiders looking in on the process. Not everyone can or even wants to be the next Bill Gates or Steve Jobs.

Some people go into business for themselves just so they can have control over their life. If you have ever been the victim of job loss or demotion, you know the value of control. If an entrepreneur makes enough money to pay the bills or buy extra things he or she couldn't otherwise afford, that may just be icing on the cake.

While entrepreneurship can be very time-consuming, at the end of the day, you are your own boss and if something else needs priority, you don't need to ask anyone for permission to change your priorities for that day, week, month or year. You know your obligations and your limits, and you can build your business around those accordingly. Being in control of your life and living without fear of losing your job can be priceless for many people. And if that is your end goal for starting your business, celebrate that accomplishment each and every day.

Conclusion

Becoming an entrepreneur is an exciting and empowering journey. No matter what your ultimate goal is, becoming dependent solely on your wit and grit is worth the big, scary risk. I remember that pivotal day when I left the safety of corporate employment to start my own law firm. I felt scared, anxious, and excited all at the same time. I watched my favorite movie, *Rocky II*, that evening, August 4, 2014, to help ignite that fire in my belly. I didn't really know where my path would lead the day I took that first step, but I was willing to walk down that path with my eyes wide open and with my mind receptive to ideas along the way.

159

Why did I do it? Because I didn't want to look back in twenty years and wonder, "*What if?*" I didn't want to feel regret. Regret, as I have learned, comes from mistakes that haunt us for life. Those mistakes can be great teachers and make us strive to do better, but they still haunt us. I did not need to be haunted by another mistake.

So, once you take that first step toward entrepreneurship, you don't need to have all the answers right then. Answers will appear when they need to, as long as you are constantly looking out for them and are asking the right questions. Make sure you have a team of advisors and friends who can help you navigate as you continue your journey. They can help you stay or change course as needed.

Don't put too much pressure on yourself, just enough to accomplish your goals, both short and long-term. If life gets too hectic, don't be afraid to ask for help or scale back. You can adjust, and you can achieve your own definition of success. Entrepreneurship is a blessing. It is a path to finding your purpose, solving life's problems and creating joy. And best of all, it can be done from anywhere.

While writing this book, my family traveled to Yellowstone National Park from our home in Wisconsin. On our return trip, we stopped in Wall, South Dakota. Anyone who has traveled East/West across South Dakota on Highway 90 has seen the multitude of billboards advertising "free ice water" and "5-cent coffee) at Wall Drug. We stopped at Wall Drug and learned the story behind the "free ice water" offer. Ted and Dorothy Hustead bought Wall Drug in 1931. Wall is in the middle of nowhere and for years, the Husteads had difficulty making ends meet because very few customers came to their drug store.

Then, one hot summer day, upon hearing noisy cars traveling on the highway, Dorothy asked the question: "What do people want when driving across the hot prairie?" Water. Ice cold water. Wall Drug could offer that to people for free. That would lead them to the store where they may buy other things. And it worked.

Wall Drug is a tourist spot now, and when we were there this past summer, it was as crowded as it was the first time I visited ten years ago.

What's Next?

In a brochure describing Wall Drug, Ted Hustead is quoted as writing the following:

> *Free Ice Water. It brought us Husteads a long way and taught me my greatest lesson, and that's that there's absolutely no place on God's earth that's Godforsaken. No matter where you live, you can succeed, because wherever you are, you can reach out to other people with something that they need!*[45]

You can do this. You should do this. Someone in the world needs your idea, and implementing your idea is why you are here. Listen to that tug. It's leading you to where you need to go.

---

[45] Wall and Water, Ted Hustead, in *Welcome to Wall Drug and the Badlands* brochure (August 21, 2020).

Afterword

I STARTED WRITING THIS BOOK AT THE same time I started Pursesuitz. I wanted to chronicle the entrepreneurship process from the very beginning to some point during the first year of a start-up. As expected, my idea for Pursesuitz evolved as I moved through the process, and so did the purpose of this book.

My initial intended audience for this book was "ambitious women," because I thought they would be the most interested in learning about the evolution of Pursesuitz. But after hearing the feedback from the focus groups about the Pursesuitz blouse and COVID-19 hitting four months into 2020, I knew the business idea needed to shift course, and so did the book. But I wasn't exactly sure how to pivot with the book.

I was about half-way through writing the book when a friend from whom I hadn't heard in nearly 20 years reached out. She was approaching her 50th birthday and had become restless. Her kids were getting older and she had been working in the same job for about 13 years. She was ready for a change. She had been following me on social media and was intrigued by my entrepreneurial ventures. She then told me she had a dream about me and when she awoke, she knew we had to reconnect.

We spoke by phone for about an hour, and during that conversation, I heard a familiar voice of inquisitiveness and yearning. She wanted to know how and why I started my business and whether it was really working for me thus far. She expressed a desire to do something similar but was unsure of the path forward. She thought that by talking to me, her own ideas could become clearer. It reminded me of what I had felt in 2014 when I started my law firm. It was a "tug" to do something more, something scary and completely out of character.

When I hung up the phone, I felt really humbled. Here was a person I had admired for a long time coming to me because she saw inspiration in what I was doing with my life. That conversation cleared the haze I had been seeing for the re-focus of my book.

This book is for would-be entrepreneurs who have some ideas of what they may like to do, but aren't sure if and how to proceed. They have a gut feeling that there is more to life than their 9-to-5 job, but are afraid of the unknown. I use my experiences with three entrepreneurial ventures—Lemonspark, the Center for Health and Wellness Law, LLC, and Pursesuitz—to lead you through the phases of entrepreneurship.

It should be noted that none of my ventures have made me a millionaire (yet), but they have brought me joy and continue to do so. Joy is how another one of my lawyer friends, Rhonda Ware of URAware Life Coaching, convincingly described success to me. The bottom line for me, and I suspect for many of the readers of this book, is to find your purpose that brings you the most joy. Life is too short to feel minimal joy. With the map I provide in this book, and my testimonials about my own ventures, you can also find your purpose and joy by heeding the call of your own "tug."

12 KEY TAKEAWAYS FROM *THE TUG*

1. You have a "Divine Design" that often flashes into your conscious mind as something that seems too good to be true. Your "tug" is leading you there.

2. Once you know your true purpose, very little can shake it from you.

3. Success is not necessarily about how quickly you achieve your goals, but how persistent you are in moving forward.

4. The law can help protect you and your idea, and a good legal partner can be priceless at some point along your entrepreneurial journey.

5. Funding does not need to be an obstacle, especially if you define your success to match your funding resources, of which there are numerous options.

6. Finding your tribe of customers or believers is critical to finding success.

7. Your biggest competition is likely yourself. See above, #1 and #2.

8. Proving to yourself and the world that your idea will work builds confidence in you, potential funders, and customers.

9. You are the brand behind your product or service. Infuse your product or service with your unique perspective and voice to help it stand out from the crowd.

10. You don't need to hire employees to have a team.

11. You don't need to spend a lot of money on paid advertising to get the word out about your product or service. Take advantage of the plentiful avenues of content marketing.

12. You are the captain of your entrepreneurial ship. You control the speed and destination, which is the beauty and thrill of the entrepreneurial journey.

ACKNOWLEDGEMENTS

THE INSPIRATION AND TENACITY FOR writing this book come from many people, and each played a significant part in seeing this book become reality. First, I credit my husband Branden Zimmerman for always believing that I can accomplish whatever I desire and that he will have my back no matter what. Thank you. Next, I want to thank my children, Patrick and Vivian, without whom I would not have the same drive to succeed. Vivian gets additional thanks for designing *The Tug*'s cover; your artistic talents continue to amaze me and I am so proud to call you my daughter. (Check out Vivian's art at www.vazlart.com.)

Also important to this book in particular are Rhonda Ware, for reaching out at the perfect moment to help me see the value in pushing forward with my idea, and Elizabeth Stone, who because of her phone call and curiosity, changed the purpose and direction of *The Tug*. Elizabeth, you gave me a concrete vision of The Tug's audience.

I would also like to thank Michaela Conley for always checking in on me and making me smile. Thank you for your friendship. Special thanks to Michelle Spehr and Kim Shaul, who offered to review the book before I sent it to the publisher.

To all those who endorsed my book: Jennifer Abernethy, Michael Barbouche, Bob Devita, Suzanne Klahr, Angus Nelson, Laura Putnam, and Rosie Ward—many thanks to you. I appreciate your willingness to vouch for my book. And thank you, Kira Henschel, for taking a chance on me to publish this book and for suggesting wonderful support people like Valerie Johnson and Elaine Meszaros, who have been so helpful in spreading the word about the book and what I do.

I would also like to thank all my colleagues at the University of Wisconsin—Milwaukee, including Jennifer Fink, Jake Lou, Priya Nambisan, Kathleen Olewinski, Gary Ross, Hanh Trinh, and Min Wu for being so supportive of all my efforts, as well as my colleagues from the Center for Health and Wellness Law: Alyssa Ehrlich, Paul Fenaroli,

Joe Forward, Tom Halloran, and Leah Ruedinger. Thank you for being such great attorneys so that the Center's clients continue to get great legal services.

Finally, I want to thank John Murray. If it hadn't been for that pivotal lunch meeting when you asked me to leave my corporate job and return to private law practice, I might never have listened to my own "tug" and started my entrepreneurial journey. I never imagined I could take such a risk or that it could fill me with so much purpose and joy.

About the Author

Barbara J. Zabawa, JD, MPH, is the founder and president of the Center for Health and Wellness Law, LLC, a law firm dedicated to improving legal access and compliance for the health and wellness industries. She is also the founder of Purseuitz, LLC, a mission-based fashion company featuring the Pocketwear Tank and that promotes gender equality. Learn more at www.pursesuitz.com. Finally, she is the founder of Lemonspark, a movement and podcast celebrating the sparks that lead people to meaningful pursuits after experiencing life's lemons. See www.lemonspark.com.

Barbara is lead author of the book, Rule the Rules on Workplace Wellness Programs, published by the American Bar Association. She is a frequent writer and speaker on health and wellness law topics, having presented for national organizations such as WELCOA, National Wellness Conference, HPLive, Healthstat University, and HERO.

She is a Clinical Assistant Professor for the University of Wisconsin–Milwaukee College of Health Sciences, Department of Health Services Administration, where she teaches graduate and undergraduate courses in health law and compliance, US healthcare and delivery, and health professions career development.

Barbara serves health and wellness professionals and organizations across the country as an advocate, a transactional lawyer, and a compliance resource. Her commitment to improving health and wellness also shows through her community service. Barbara founded the Wellness Compliance Institute, a nonprofit organization that seeks to improve wellness program and activity compliance. She also serves on the Board of Directors for the National Wellness Institute.

She is licensed to practice law in both Wisconsin and New York.

CONTACT INFORMATION:

Emails:
- bzabawa@wellnesslaw.com
- bzabawa@pursesuitz.com
- barbz@lemonspark.com

Websites:
- www.barbarazabawa.com
- www.wellnesslaw.com
- www.pursesuitz.com
- www.lemonspark.com

Twitter:
- @wellnessatty
- @pursesuitz
- @lemonsparkstories

LinkedIn: www.linkedin.com/in/barbarazabawa

Instagram:
- Wellnessattorney
- Pursesuitz
- Lemonsparkstories

Facebook:
- @centerforhealthandwellnesslaw
- @pursesuitz
- @lemonspark

Made in the USA
Monee, IL
31 July 2021

74654425R10101